*To my husband, Alan,
the MK who has lovingly
shared his life with me.*

10.36

96593

Table of Contents

LINCOLN CHRISTIAN COLLEGE AND SEMINARY

DON'T PIG OUT ON JUNK FOOD

The MK'S Guide to Survival in the U.S.

Alma Daugherty Gordon

Copyright © 1993 by Alma Daugherty Gordon
ISBN 9617751-1-4

Published by Evangelical Missions Information Service
Box 794, Wheaton, Ill. 60189
(708) 653-2158
Printed in the United States of America

All rights reserved. No part of this publication may be reproduced, stored in a retrieval system, or transmitted in any form or by any means—electronic, mechanical, photocopy, recording or any other—without the prior written permission of the publisher. The only exception is brief quotations in printed reviews.

The Evangelical Missions Information Service (EMIS) publishes *Evangelical Missions Quarterly* and *Pulse* newsletter. The purpose of EMIS is to inform, motivate, and equip missionaries and help shape the theories, values, and practices of the evangelical missionary enterprise.

Other EMIS publications: *Overcoming Missionary Stress*, by Dr. Marjory Foyle ($9.95); *Kids of the Kingdom*, a 32-page bibliography of books, articles, and theses pertaining to missionary children ($5.00).

For further information, write: EMIS, P.O. Box 794, Wheaton, Ill. 60189.

Library of Congress Cataloging-in-Publication Data

Gordon, Alma Daugherty, 1933-
    Don't pig out on junk food: the MK's guide to survival in the
U.S./Alma Daugherty Gordon.
    p.   cm.
    Includes bibliographical references and index.
    ISBN 0-9617751-1-4 (pbk.) : $9.95
    1. Children of missionaries.   2. Reverse culture shock.
I. Title.
BV2094.5.G67   1993
266' .0083--dc20   93-34545
                                        CIP

Illustrations by Marcia d'Haese

Worksheets by Sandra Gordon

Cover design and illustration copyright © 1993 by David LaPlaca

Chapter 5: Relationships

Chapter 6: Tools That Have
Helped Upon Cross-Cultural Entry

Appendices

Resources

Foreword

To be born and nurtured in a land whose culture is alien to the developed Western world is not a choice an MK (Missionary Kid) can make. But it is more than likely that the majority of those who have grown up in strange and exotic lands consider themselves among the most fortunate of the world's citizens. The advantages are so numerous, the traumas so rare and so generally exaggerated, that only an exceptional MK will express strong negative reactions toward the circumstances foisted upon him in his formative years.

When the benefits are listed, such as knowing a foreign language well enough to speak it without an accent, in addition to gaining positive interracial relationships that promote open-mindedness and keen sensibility toward other cultures, the values form an inestimable treasure. There is the comprehension and appreciation of radically different value systems, the independence that comes in the wake of globe-trotting, all on top of the scintillating memories of geography gained through one's eyes rather than through boring school lectures. When one considers beyond all of this the maturity gained from spending time with mission leaders and nationals "that make things happen," one should dispel all doubt about the best education available anywhere being the mission field.

But there are other factors that need examining, as Alma Gordon does in this book. She openly discusses what all of us who grew up far from the original habitat of our parents understood, however vaguely. Missionary life can be painful and even traumatic. While the long list of advantages are intellectual, enhancing mind and experience, these other factors relate to the heart and emotions.

It often hurts to be frequently uprooted, to be forcibly separated from parents and friends, to study in distant missionary schools. Nagging questions haunt lonely hours. Where does one belong, the "homeland," or land a progenitor has chosen to live in? Which is my own culture, the native variety or the sanitized veneer of Western culture one's parents value so highly?

Then there are life crises which call for a double portion of God's grace and human understanding. My own were two. Sitting on the second class wooden seat of the train which chugged slowly along the clacking rails, I felt sure the old security of home was receding forever. Barely seven years old, I knew that there would be no superficial easy solution to the feeling of inner loss. I would have to face it largely on my own in the impersonal institutional atmosphere of the mission school. Homesickness, gnawing within, became for the first time a felt reality. After all, who could help even if I were not too proud to unleash the pent-up resentment created deep within by the sense of loss I could not explain? However, the crisis lost substance and vanished.

The second critical period of my life lasted much longer, a full year, provoked by mother and dad leaving for Bolivia for a seven-year term, while I remained behind with brother and sister to survive in a prison-like "home" for missionary children. The routine was highly structured, the food sparse, the work uninteresting. Worst of all, I was thirteen and an awkward adolescent. But God is equal to every challenge. A year later joy had replaced despair. Never again did I have to face that emotional vacuum, wondering who I was, nor why I was so unhappy and felt so lost and aimless. Of course, young people don't have to be MKs to experience such traumas, but they were well nigh inevitable in the hoary past when children left home at an early age, parents remained largely incommunicado, and furloughs were far between. Rarer still, in my experience, was the surrogate parent or counselor who could convince me that he really cared. But it couldn't have been all that bad, or three out of us four MKs would not have chosen missions as a career.

This book will easily convince you that life is different now. People are not only concerned, but working hard, to find solutions to MK crises. To all my MK friends I would say, "You are more fortunate than ever to be a member of so privileged a club!"

—*Russell Shedd*

7

Preface

The word "missionary" brings to mind travel, exotic faraway places, other cultures and languages—all of them valid images. Any adults who live in other cultures will broaden their perspectives, but their children will inevitably be a blend of cultures. They can be called Trans-Cultural Kids (TCKs).

A TCK is an individual who, having spent a significant part of the developmental years in a culture other than the parents' culture, develops a sense of relationship to both. MKs, as well as children of business, military, and diplomatic people who live abroad, become these culture-blend persons who often contribute in unique and creative ways to society as a whole.

The individual blend will vary, depending on such factors as the intensity of exposure to a second or third culture, at what ages a child comes into contact with a culture other than that of the parents, and the amount of time a young person spends within a second or third culture. The TCK's roots are not embedded in a place, but in people, with a sense of belonging growing out of relationships to others of similar experience.

Because of frequent changes in geographic location, a TCK tends to be a very independent person, often a loner. That self-reliance can be turned into an asset as the young person matures, contributing to the TCK's ability to make decisions and to exercise leadership. However, self-reliance is but one step away from isolation. If a TCK does not need or trust anyone, he or she cannot function in society in a healthy way.

A TCK can never change back into a monocultural person. Parents of TCKs can return "home" to their country of origin, but the children, enriched by having shared life in their formative years with another people, will find characteristics of both cultures in their very being. Acceptance of this fact frees TCKs to be uniquely themselves. In fact, TCKs have tools to be the cultural brokers of the future.

Even though this book has been written especially for missionary families and their MKs (missionary kids), other TCKs have been kept in mind as well. With slight adjustments, the material can be useful to all families in transition. The book focuses on the responses by MKs themselves to four questions in a Missionary Information Bureau questionnaire:

8

1. "What would you like to have known before reentering your parents' home country?"
2. "What tools (conferences, books, clubs, articles, people, etc.) did you find were most helpful in your cross-cultural entry (reentry?)"
3. "What advice would you give another MK preparing to return to the parents' home country for college or work?"
4. "What suggestions would you make to mission boards or missionary parents concerning rearing children, MK schooling, and general missionary family life?"

More than 100 responses were received from MKs, ranging in age from 12 to 78. Their statements are grouped throughout the book under the heading, "MKs SAY." From these comments, parents and their MKs can sense what others have encountered and felt in cross-cultural transitions.

There have been many difficult, and sometimes hurtful, happenings in the lives of some MKs. Except for two respondents, however, all of the MKs interviewed in person or through the questionnaire wholeheartedly stated that they would not trade their MK experiences for anything else. (Our special thanks to all the MKs who enthusiastically responded to the MIB questionnaire.)

Information also came from many gatherings of mission leaders, missionary parents, educators, and groups of MKs themselves. Other important sources were the ICMK-Quito (International Conference on Missionary Kids) held in Ecuador, January, 1987; the MK Seminar presented by Interfaces (International Family and Children's Educational Services) at the Overseas Ministries Study Center, New Haven, Conn., November, 1988; and the ICMK-Nairobi, held in Kenya, November, 1989. The author participated in all of these. More recently she has been working with missionary families from the young sending churches of the third world, which has added a new dimension to this material.

The answers to our questionnaire determined the outline of this book, which covers the following major areas of importance to MKs and their families: The preparation a family can make so that its members feel less stress at cross-cultural entry times is the topic of the first and second chapters. Self-identity of an MK is discussed in the third chapter. The areas of itineration, child abuse, loneliness, homesickness, suicide, and faith are touched upon, as well as the advantages of being an MK.

The fourth chapter emphasizes one of the most mentioned topics in our survey: how to do various things. Included is information that is often needed on specific "how-to's" and some differences in cultural habits. The fifth chapter explores relationships, the key to a positive adjustment.

It includes many hints sent in by MKs and has some suggestions on setting up a support group.

In chapter six, there is a list of "tools that have helped" many an MK in cross-cultural entry. Topics included are counseling, crucial areas such as drugs, AIDS, and alcohol, and a section on the advantages of a missionary family. In general lines, the early chapters apply more to families with younger children, and the later chapters to those with older children.

Throughout the book are suggestions for concrete ways a family can explore and learn about a particular topic that affects the life of an MK. The MK anecdotes at the beginning of each chapter are all true stories. The work sheets and "Questions for Reflection" at the end of each chapter are based on information in that chapter. In this way the reader has at least two choices of ways to discuss and apply the material to his or her own situation. Be sure to use the appendices and resources at the end of the book.

The words *"cross-cultural entry,"* also called *"reentry,"* are used to mean the transition time when a TCK has left the host country and is first experiencing the parents' home country. This is most crucial at the time a young person leaves home to live on his or her own at college, or to work. It is, however, meant also to include shorter periods of time during which a family travels back to the parents' home country. Actually, everyone changing from one culture to another and then back again will experience some need for a cross-cultural entry adjustment at each change.

Coming out of the author's own TCKness (fourth generation overseas and having reared six fifth-generation MKs to adulthood), this book seeks to add to the growing amount of research being done over the last decade on cross-cultural influences on children reared overseas. The common experiences of hundreds of MKs are expressed and can be used as a resource for helping parents and other adults prepare their children for the special challenges and transitions in life.

It is hoped that positive problem-prevention programs will be the norm for those getting ready to live overseas. Prefield orientation is the ideal time to begin work with parents and their families on cross-cultural issues. However, there will always be more to learn as missionary life is a continual crossing of cultural boundaries.

A book like this is never really finished, for people keep coming up with new and better ways to handle life. We would like to hear from you. Let us know what is particularly helpful, and do share your experiences. Not all responses that are quoted here are applicable to any one person. Pick and choose what seems to work best for you.

Both the problems and the helps related to cross-cultural entry into the parents' home country have been emphasized. This is, of course, one-sided, since all TCKs are a blend of cultures, and this book does not address helping TCKs become a comfortable part of the host culture.

Perhaps another book will follow. To any of you who are TCKs and ready to give up, DON'T. Read this book, or write or call. We will listen.

Alma D. Gordon
Rua Cambuci do Vale 597/106
São Paulo, SP, BRAZIL
04805-110
Telephone (011) 55-11-247-3232

ACKNOWLEDGEMENT. The Missionary Information Bureau (MIB) in São Paulo, Brazil, has been of inestimable help to missionary families since its founding in 1964. The first edition of this book, *The MK Challenge* (1989), was in great part due to MIB's encouragement and help. Special thanks to the MIB Board and to Diane Bechtel.

MARCIA d'HAESE

Introduction

In a few months our family would leave Africa and return to the United States for a year's furlough. We wanted to make sure that our three young sons would feel at home in the different environment, so we carefully picked out up-to-date clothes in the Sears catalog and received them in plenty of time for the big trip.

Our first glimpse of "Lady Liberty" and a whiff of the cold, crisp air set our hearts to singing, "Home, home, home!" Once out of customs, we called to the boys to follow as we hurried along the walkway, anxious at last to see family. With so many emotions tumbling in our hearts, we were glad that we didn't need to worry about how the boys looked. They looked just as American as any boys around.

At first we thought the people going by were very friendly, smiling at us that way. Then the extra attention seemed a little strange, rather out of the ordinary. Confused, we slackened our pace and glanced back at the boys following us. Sure enough, they were dressed in the latest American styles—but they proudly carried their suitcases on their heads!

This story superbly illustrates what life is like for an MK (Missionary Kid), who can also be considered a TCK (Trans-Cultural Kid). Even though growing up surrounded by more than one culture can at times be very confusing, most MKs have a very positive outlook on life, as seen by the following responses in which MKs offer advice to other MKs facing cross-cultural entry.

Advice from MKs to MKs:

✔ *"Be yourself and ready for lots of changes."*

✔ *"Don't take yourself too seriously; laugh at your mistakes."*

- ✔ *"It's OK to be different; don't be afraid to be out of it."*
- ✔ *"Enjoy the good of both cultures, the new things you have an opportunity to learn."*
- ✔ *"Bite your tongue for awhile and learn. Look for good."*
- ✔ *"Keep a good attitude; be cordial and understanding rather than critical."*
- ✔ *"Don't feel sorry for yourself. Decide to adjust, make the best of it and see the transition as a challenge."*
- ✔ "Be content, thankful and positive."
- ✔ "Look, listen, ask, get a feel for, enjoy!"

Advice from MKs to parents and leaders:
- ✔ *"Encourage MKs to be content wherever they are."*

"Laugh at your mistakes."

Encouraging MKs to be content wherever they are really is the secret, and yet it does not happen overnight or without effort. The process of helping a TCK become a creative and mature adult has many more helps today as knowledge and experience are pooled. It is important to remember that good parenting is not a matter of geography. There are few hard and fast rules, but there are directions that should be taken. MK ministries are worthwhile to help enhance advantages and minimize disadvantages for the over 30,000 MKs out there, according to Mu Kappa International. The following poem, written by an MK, is a beautiful word picture describing MKs.

Travelers

For the 1987 U.S. reunions of
Central School for Missionaries' Children and
The American School of Kinshasa, Zaire

Even those who've stopped in one place,
snug in Georgia, Saskatchewan, or
Indiana, are travelling. Night in Richmond, this one
dreams a steamship heaving across the grey
Atlantic. Pausing at the rocky, glaring Canaries,
he looks for yellow songsters, finds
seagulls, and sails on. He wakes up sobbing at Matadi
docks, and his wife turns, mumbles,
"What is it, sweetheart?" and sleeps again.
Another, walking home in Denver: the first raindrops
splat on dry lawns and road, and the damp, dusty scent
takes her up, hurls her into Africa, end of dry season.
She breathes it in, in, and sighs it out.
Raises her umbrella, never explains.
Dry brown hyacinths on a Florida beach raise cliffs
for him, Moanda in moonlight, green water
turned muddy. One dreams a sentry's fire,
puffs the gourd water-pipe and coughs himself awake
muttering Tshiluba he's tried to forget.
Another swims upriver in her sleep, stroking
against the current, never moving forward. Voices warn
of crocodiles, and she laughs.

Some travel back, hoping
to find home. But even in Africa, you must make a place
for who you are now, not just your father's son,
your mother's daughter. Little time, now,
for rivers, trees and animals that made your childhood
paradise. The jungle hides rebels; hungry, bored soldiers
block the roads; no parts for your car, nor medicines
for your patients' incurable diseases . . .
Grown up, you no longer find breakdown in a sandpit
amusing. You're old and strong enough now
to have to help dig it out.
We are still traveling,
even in the PTA, even as our children watch TV
cartoons and play with GI Joes, video games, Legos,
and a father remembers palmwood cars and helicopters,
hot afternoons in a high mango-tree clubhouse.
A mother remembers books by lanternlight,
a small, clean monkey asleep, hugging her arm.
Would they give their children those things, if
they could? And would they send them away
to live and conspire and laugh with other children,
to cry alone, to be taught and mothered by others?

And some travel on
from state to state, country to country, leaving
friends and lovers, being left, and moving again.
They don't need to explain any more. Somewhere
Congo/Zaire merges with Kenya with Rhode Island
with Côte d'Ivoire with Louisiana with Belgium with
Vietnam. Now and then we meet and embrace, and let
go again.

When we come together, we form our own nation
of travelers, of in-betweens. Even where we've blended, stopped
trying to explain, we meet our own and know
each other—this one understands, we speak the same
memories, dream ourselves in the same overloaded truck
rattling and bumping along in a cloud of dust as we sing.

Copyright © 1989 Beth Rambo

1

Family Preparation
For Cross-Cultural Entry

If God has called us to both parenting and ministry then he gives us the grace to do both well. Not family versus ministry, but family in ministry.

—David Pollock

I was ten years old, and my brother seven, when we arrived in Miami with our missionary parents. Our family had been on the mission field for the past six years. As soon as we kids could get away, we scampered off, intent on planning a strategy for handling this new, and to us frightening, world.

"We won't speak English," we agreed. "Our friends speak Portuguese!"

That settled, we squared our shoulders and ambled back to the large group of strangers that called themselves family. All through the day we used Portuguese to answer questions and asked for what we wanted through our parents. At times we noticed Mom and Dad looking at us quizzically.

"What's wrong with those kids?" our parents wondered. "They can speak perfectly good English."

Without realizing what we were doing, the next day we started using English. After all, it was useful, and this new place began to seem interesting and maybe even fun.

The kids in this story undoubtedly needed some way to deal with what seemed an overpowering situation. They chose language as a way to stand together. However, their transition might have been made more enjoyable by planning weeks ahead of the trip. Their arrival could have been role-played, with the inclusion of relatives, environment, and language. Preparation does not eliminate all of the hurts, but it surely lessens fear, embarrassment, and awkwardness experienced in changing from one culture to another.

For many years much effort has been put into preparing families to live overseas. Only recently has there been interest in, and studies on, the effects of the stress of coming back again. In fact, we are realizing that while a family is in another country for two or four years, those they left behind have also been changing and growing, making a total gap of four or eight years. Coming back together again can be made much easier by good preparation.

"Parents can be too involved in
the ministry and ignore their kids."

What Parents Need to Know

In answer to, "What would you like to have known before cross-cultural entry?" MKs stated the following:

✔ *"Parents can be too involved in their ministry and ignore their kids. Take a vital interest in your kids' schooling and lives (even when they are away from home)."*

✔ *"More about 18-year-old cultural America and the various directions—besides missionary and church worker—open to people my age."*

✔ *"That adjustment to college is a bigger adjustment than to the 'home' country."*

✔ *"That help would be needed during cross-cultural reentry, and not only prior to it."*

✔ *"To expect depression and loneliness as a normal part of transition."*

✔ *"That my parents didn't know the U.S. that I came to."*

✔ *"Healthy family life must be a priority; remember, the MK will adjust as well as the parents do. Plan one day off each week for a family day."*

Accurate information could have helped all of these MKs and their families.

What Parents Can do

Keep in touch with parent's home culture. Here are some suggestions:

1. Subscribe to a news magazine (*U.S.News and World Report, Time, The Economist,* etc.); a family magazine (*Better Homes & Gardens, Good Housekeeping, Highlights,* etc.); a Christian magazine (*Christian Century, Christianity Today, Campus Life,* etc.).

2. Missionary families can each order different magazines and share them with other families.

3. Ask friends and relatives to send you videos of programs or films they feel depict the parents' home country society: sports, popular television shows, etc.

4. Discuss with the family cultural trends and current news events of the world and of the parents' home country.

Practice Listening

In their responses, MKs repeatedly were concerned about their parents' over-involvement in their ministry. Whether on the field or during furloughs—while the MK is still home or after leaving for school or work—many MKs feel left out of their parents' main objective in life. What they are saying is expressed in the following anonymous poem:

> When I ask you to listen to me
> And you start giving advice
> You have not done what I asked.
> When I ask you to listen to me
> And you begin to tell me why I shouldn't feel that way
> You are trampling on my feelings.
> When I ask you to listen to me
> And you feel you have to do something to solve my problem,
> You have failed me, strange as that may seem.
> Listen! All I asked was that you listen.
> Not talk or do—just hear me.[1]

Listening, hearing someone, is not an easy task. It takes a lot of practice, and not surprisingly, all of us get better at it the more we do it.

MKs Say

As a family, discuss the ideas found throughout this book in the sections titled, "MKs SAY." All of these statements have been made by MKs.

Remember:
1. Be a good listener.
2. Draw your children into the conversation.
3. Show them you are interested in, and understand, how they feel.

Plan:
1. Give each quotation enough discussion time.
2. Take notes as you discuss quotations.
3. As a family, make plans to do things that your discussions indicate might be helpful. For example, after discussing the last quotation under MKs say to MKs below, your children could make a list of their friends and send them their new address.

MKs say to MKs:

✔ *"Keep in touch with your family, listen to their advice. Learn to write letters (to other than family, too). Be open with your parents about how you are feeling."*

✔ *"Get involved with hobbies—play baseball or master computers, develop interests and skills in transferable activities."*

✔ *"Get as much information on various colleges as possible; discover the range of career options and training needed—do lots of research; learn all you can about the place you are going to be."*

✔ *"Plan time in the U.S. before school starts for job and friends; earn money and save for extra expenses. Take time to travel and reacquaint yourself; go to a cross-cultural entry seminar. Some MKs may be helped by spending one semester in the U.S. before beginning college or by planning parents' furlough to coincide with cross-cultural-entry."*

✔ *"Distribute your address among friends."*

MKs say to parents and missions:

✔ *"Rural MKs should have city experience before leaving home. Don't try to raise kids in the tribes. They need to know the world they will go to."*

✔ *"Don't feel guilty for raising your kids as MKs. They have many advantages."*

✔ *"Listen to your children; encourage questions and the expression of feelings. Frankly discuss problems, fears and expectations."*

✔ *"Raise children to be at home in both countries; help them to become involved in the national context and language, and in your ministry."*

✔ *"Help your family keep in touch with the U.S., your friends and relatives there."*

✔ *"Help kids learn to be independent before leaving home. Provide driver's training and consider transportation needs while in college."*

✔ *"Read them Oliver Twist, Mother Goose, Aesop's Fables; discuss American events at the supper table."*

✔ *"It is very helpful to have at least one parent accompany the MK to college to help open a bank account, etc."*

✔ *"A year-long furlough during teen years or around cross-cultural entry time is helpful. During furlough, plan family times for growing closer as a family and for passing on American heritage."*

✔ *"The importance of formal education during the years on the mission field is overrated. Really important are books, interested adults and peers, either American or national."*

✔ *"Schooling decisions should be family decisions and not mission decisions, with educational options provided. In home-schooling there should be enough help provided in the home so that both parents can be involved in ministry."*

✔ *"Boarding schools should be discouraged, and avoided before the teen years."*

✔ *"Don't feel parents need to leave the field to make a home in the U.S. for college kids. They might be better off without that sacrifice."*

Most of the MKs' suggestions are not difficult to carry out and can help a young person feel more at ease in a new environment. Notice that some suggestions seem to conflict with others. Needs vary. What would be best for your family?

One of the very best ways to help your children grasp the world beyond your surroundings is to read to them. Books in your home country language bring your children into contact with your native tongue, and with aspects of your culture and heritage as well. Besides, the togetherness of these special reading times builds memories, love of learning, and a sense of stability in your child.

An important factor in helping MKs to grow up is to be able to distinguish between the petty and the profound. Are the MK's troubling moments due to normal adolescence or transient upsets over changing locations which could be felt by anyone in the same situation? Listening goes a long way in helping determine how much help an MK needs.

Listening and sharing need to be a two-way street. When parents express some of their own fears and struggles in the crossing between cultures, the children can realize their uneasiness is quite natural. The family can join together in helping each other over the rough spots, the children being helpers as well as receivers. A side benefit of this openness will be that the MKs will see a role model in action of how to handle fear and struggling rather than how to hide them, pretending on the surface that all is well.

The MK who suggested that the family take a vital interest in the young person, even when away from home, hit upon a raw nerve for many parents. (See "What parents need to know," p. 22.) Most often, sending kids far away at relatively early ages is very difficult for the parents. Much more so than kids realize. It sometimes happens that in order to cope with the hurting, a parent will choose to pretend for awhile that the child does not exist. Working hard and not thinking about the child far away makes life more bearable. But the message the child receives is, "Your parents don't care about you. They have forgotten you."

 ALERT! You must not send someone to meet your homecoming MKs. Welcome them yourself. Then listen all night if they want to talk.

Missing Your Kids?

1. **Cry.** It's OK to shed a few tears when you say good-by. Your child needs to know you care.
2. **Pray.**
   (a) <u>For yourself</u>. God will send comfort in unexpected ways. Look for it.
   (b) <u>For your children</u>. Collect Bible promises and trust your heavenly Father to keep them.
3. **Communicate.**
   (a) <u>By letters and fax and "care" packages</u>. (Include clothing, favorite foods, study supplies, etc.) These minister to your kids, but they also can soothe your heart as you do something for your MK.

(b) <u>By phone</u>. Hearing your child's voice on special days like birth-days, Mother's Day, Christmas, or every couple of months helps you to feel closer.

(c) <u>By visits.</u> One family arranged for at least one parent to visit each of their "away" kids once a year. Sometimes this was in conjunction with business trips, sometimes it was simply making the rounds of the kids. Sleeping in college dorms, eating in the cafeteria, going to classes with your MKs and meeting some of their friends gives you a new appreciation for your child's life and struggles.

4. **Be thankful.** Thank God that your MK has matured and is able to start out on his or her own. With God's help, you have done a good job. Be thankful for the growing busy childhood years, and now look forward to hearing about and watching your young person become a creative and interesting adult. Your own horizons will broaden with your MK's. It's an exciting journey.

5. **Act.** You now have more time. You can sit and mope, or you can:

(a) Invest your time and love into the lives of children and young people around you.

(b) Look at your marriage partner with new eyes and find creative ways to communicate.

(c) Develop a natural gift you had set aside during those active family years.

When you realize that your children may think you don't care for them, responsible love will win out in most parents, and the situation can be corrected. Today's technology is a great asset in communicating over long distances. Ease of letters (even from some tribal areas), telephone, radio, photographs and even video and fax can do a lot to keep families in contact. More frequent travel has become accessible in cost and time, enabling parents to go to the MKs and the kids to come home. The central question now is priorities. It is not an easy question, but it is possible for each family to find adequate answers.

Keeping in Touch

Here are some ways to keep in touch with faraway children while you are still on the field. Some of these suggestions are fast and easy, yet they will be greatly appreciated.

1. **Letters.** Write every week or two. (See Chapter 5.)

2. **Phone.** Use AT&T, MCI, etc. credit cards and save money.[2] Use a timer to keep track of the time.

3. **Fax.** Take a cartoon from the newspaper, glue it to a sheet of paper, add a few comments and fax it. Many offices provide this service. It is a fast way to get documents and special occasion thoughts to your MKs.
4. **Cassettes.** Take five or ten minutes to record an oral letter on an audio cassette. Sit down and do it, or dictate it into a hand-held tape recorder as you drive, perhaps giving a blow-by-blow account of your day-to-day ministry. In a few minutes you have shared the news and your MK hears your voice, too.
5. **Photos and Video.** Set up the video camera on a tripod and film a family dinner. Keep a camera ready for those funny or memorable moments.
6. **TV.** Record TV shows from the host country.
7. **News.** Send articles from local papers or magazines.
8. **Music.** Send taped music from the host country.
9. **Ham Radio.** There is a Christian network willing to help you. Talk to a ham radio operator about it.

A person usually becomes a part of the society within which she or he comes of age. The transition from child to adult and the accompanying choices, such as profession and mate, are colored by the surrounding society. This needs to be taken into account as your family makes plans with your MKs. It should be pointed out that if the child expects to remain in the host country (and to emphasize the host culture in that MK), then she or he should not be sent back to the parents' home country in her or his late teens.

Another long-term preparation to consider is to return to the same place each furlough. If a family is in the same place every few years, friendships can be maintained and these will be a great source of stability and help to MKs living on their own for the first time. Cultivating home country friends for all of the family members helps provide a smoother cross-cultural transition.

Thousands of missionaries from dozens of countries are rearing families in host cultures all over the world. The missionary task is international, not colonial. This means that the support system for the missionary community should be concentrating on the beauty of the variety in cultures and helping families prepare their children to handle well their blend.

It is not odd to "enter" and "reenter."
It is a mark of our times.

End Notes

1. An anonymous poem in *Care of the Mentally Ill*, by Sharon Dreyer Lester.
2. AT&T Calling Card, P.O. Box 41970, Kansas City, Mo. 64141. Call collect (816) 654-6004, or toll free (800) 882-2273. MCI Telecommunications, 230 Schilling Plaza South, Hunt Valley, Md. 21031. Ask for information on "non-subscriber card."

"Raise children to be at home in both countries."

Questions For Reflection

These questions can be used to help parents apply some of the material in the chapter to their own situation.

1. Why do you think the two children in the story at the beginning of the chapter would not speak English?

2. What would you have done if they were your kids?

3. What preparation for living overseas can you remember receiving? What was especially useful? Was any of it useful in your reentry?

4. How did you feel when you first arrived back in your home country?

5. If you had children when you reentered, what do you remember of their reactions to the new environment?

6. What had changed in your home country?

7. What new words were being used?

8. What do you think is more important: your work or your family?

9. Should children be raised by the rules of the host culture or the parents' home culture?

10. List ten important items (in order of their importance) that a missionary family with children should take to the field.

11. What is the ideal time between furloughs? How long should a furlough be?

12. How can you stay in contact with your children who are off at school?

Work Sheets

Work sheets can provide a focus for advance preparation for cross-cultural entry. Make a copy of the work sheets for each member of the family so that each one can think about and answer the questions that are of interest. Plan a family sharing time once a week to talk about the issues raised. Tackle only a few items each time. Listen to each other.

Exercise 1: BLAST OFF!

List ten important items (in order of importance) that a missionary family with children should take to the field.

_____ _____

_____ _____

_____ _____

_____ _____

_____ _____

Name nine new words you encountered upon cross-cultural entry.

_____ _____

_____ _____

_____ _____

_____ _____

_____

Name eight changes you encountered in your home country upon your return.

_____   _____

_____   _____

_____   _____

_____   _____

List seven ways you would stay in contact with your children off at school.

_____   _____

_____   _____

_____   _____

_____

Give six reasons why (check and answer A or B)

A. Your work is more important than your family.

_____   _____

_____   _____

_____   _____

B. Your family is more important than your work.

_____   _____

_____   _____

_____   _____

What five preparations for living overseas did you receive? Was any of it useful? Did any of it apply also to your return?

_____

_____

_____

_____

_____

Label four feelings you had upon arriving back in your home country.

_____   _____

_____   _____

Give three reactions your children had (if applicable).

_____   _____

_____

What two numbers would complete the following:

The ideal time between furloughs is _____(years, months, days).

Furloughs should last _____(years, months, days).

Give one reason why you want your children to (check A, B or C):

_____ A. Be truly bicultural.
_____ B. Reflect more of the host culture.
_____ C. Reflect more of your home culture.

Reason:_____

_____

_____

2

Preparation
For Cross-Cultural
Entry Starts Early

"Rural MKs should have city
experience before leaving home."

If you plant for a year, plant rice;
If you plant for ten years, plant a tree;
If you plant for hundreds of years, plant people.
—Korean proverb

———

I *was a student who lived with my missionary family overseas. As I prepared for college, I tackled some difficult correspondence courses, among them chemistry. The experiments were the trickiest part, because often assumptions about the conditions made my experiments invalid.*

One of the lessons asked me to determine whether there was any dust in the air. I was to set out a pie pan with an inch of water, and, after a week, observe whether or not dust skimmed the surface. ·

That same afternoon, though, the water had evaporated, and an inch of thick red dust filled the pan. A hot, dry climate, unpaved streets, and windstorms were the deciding factors in declaring the experiment finished. I might not even be able to find the pan in a week!

———

Education

Most of the MK responses about education had to do with schooling on the field. The variety of suggestions (**MKs Say**, p. 42) illustrate the many possibilities for MK education. No single choice is always the best. The important factors are each person's academic needs, thorough research as a family, and an open mind toward possible changes along the educational road.

Schools require students to learn to handle words, and if they don't like words, they are out of it. However, not all MKs find studies easy.

Some have other important and very necessary gifts. A family needs to be realistic in helping a young person decide how to prepare best for life's work.

We give a lot of lip service to "all honorable work is of equal value in society," but in our actions we imply that the most important work has to do with books and words and thoughts. This is unfair to those whose gifts are to make something beautiful with their hands, or to care lovingly for a child. SIL (Summer Institute of Linguistics) is a prime example of the need for both "word" people and "support" people. Translators could not function if someone weren't doing such things as monitoring the radio or buying supplies in town.

Suggestions:

1. Consider each person's academic needs individually.
2. Do thorough research.
3. Do research jointly as a family.
4. Keep an open mind toward possible changes along the educational road.

Here are some ways parents can help their children, even young children, to prepare for a career:

1. Help the child in a weak area, such as math.
2. Support an interest, such as history, by providing books and periodicals, and reading the newspaper together.
3. See your MKs as individuals and encourage their contributions to your family life, such as curiosity about how some machine works.
4. Learn with your children about specific careers, what preparation they require, and what tasks are involved.
5. Make sure your children understand that being a missionary is not the only way to serve the Lord.
6. Encourage your children to see how different careers can help people.

MKs need adults around who will encourage them to excel and be faithful at whatever skills God has given them. Teaching your children at home means more than just book learning. Paul Nelson, former superintendent of children's education for Wycliffe Bible Translators, and now president of Missionary Internship, said, "I've seen families keep their children home for study, but they don't even go on picnics together!"

HOME SCHOOLING: In home schooling, for official recognition of your child's grade level, contact your home state or country for specific educational requirements.

Often you must make a choice between staying at home and going away to study. Boarding schools have as many advocates as critics. The crucial factor seems to be the houseparents. If they are loving, kind, and wise, a child almost always has a positive experience. Other factors are: (1) the child's age—many MKs and educators suggest waiting until high school; (2) the presence of siblings; (3) the individual make-up of the MK. It is important to make sure your children do not feel you are glad to get rid of them. The "Three R's" ("Reading, 'Riting and 'Rithmetic") and TLC ("Tender, Loving Care") go hand in hand.

A furlough period, and going to college, present different educational needs in preparing children for cross-cultural entry.

Cross-Cultural Entry For Furlough

Schooling Choices: Advantages and Disadvantages

1. **English curriculum school** (boarding-Christian-secular). A standard English curriculum and a calendar patterned after the home country allow the student to transfer back and forth with a minimum of educational problems. Often the school is far from the parents' working field, which means the children must leave home at an early age, or the parents must move closer to the school.

2. **Home study.** Many excellent courses are available, based on standard English curriculums; easy transfer back and forth. Educational materials for home study can be used in at least two ways:

   (a) By matriculating the student in a correspondence school that sets standards and schedules to be followed. Tests and projects are graded at the school. Mail can be expensive and mail service is sometimes unreliable, but this system provides the home student with professional teaching help.

38

(b) Correspondence schools and other educational institutions will provide educational materials for students to use at home completely on their own. This is less expensive and the family is free to decide what is best for an individual student. It does take the parents time and effort to oversee the schooling. This choice also requires that the student take educational placement tests upon return to the home country, in order to fit into the existing educational system. In home study, students may lack experience in listening to the teacher, taking notes, giving oral reports, and working with peers. They may, however, do better at self-study, a useful tool in college.

3. **Host country school.** Provides peer group interaction. A good school offers a rigorous academic atmosphere. This gives the student a bi-cultural base for understanding the world and more fully integrates the family in the community.

Students may have deficiencies in English grammar and literature, and in history and geography of the home country. These can be supplemented by the parents.

Transfers between countries need to be planned around differences in school-year calendars. The student may lose half or all of a school year, but gains much more in multicultural experience.

Cross-Cultural Entry For college

There are four major steps:
1. The process of preparing the student to function independently. (See topics such as decision-making, financial management, crisis handling, etc.).

2. The process of choosing a college or other educational institution in the home country. International schools and libraries in consulates will have reference books listing colleges. The school guidance counselor can provide useful, up-to-date information for families in the process of making a decision about schooling. The bibliography in this book will also give some references. In making plans for post-high school study a young person can be better prepared for educational choices by taking a skills inventory test which can point to a student's interests and abilities, strengths and weaknesses. This testing could be done on a furlough, or at an international school, or through a correspondence course. Helping a young person think

about his or her abilities, likes, and gifts is good preparation for choosing a college and a major area of study.

3. The process of applying to a college. Again, a guidance counselor in an international school nearest you can be of great help in this process. When writing to colleges, clearly state you are a native speaker of English and a U.S. citizen (if indeed you are) in order to be sent correct material. Most colleges have a 1-800 (toll free) admissions phone number. If you are in the U.S., use these numbers to gather information. Colleges willingly send information to any address, even overseas.

4. Making sure the student has access to such tests as: PSAT (Preliminary Scholastic Aptitude Test), SAT (Scholastic Aptitude Test), ACT (American College Testing), and even TOEFL (Test of English as a Foreign Language) if needed. These tests are given mid-high school on, and different ones are required by different schools.

SAT and ACT—Most schools in the U.S. require the SAT (Scholastic Aptitude Test) or the ACT (American College Testing) results as part of the application process. Outside the USA, information and schedules for this testing service are generally available through international schools, military schools, and/or consulates.

In preparing an MK for college, it is helpful to remember that PSAT and SAT scores are based on verbal and math scores, both subjects which can be learned in almost any setting. It is encouraging to know that an MK does not need a lot of fancy courses to compete for college places. Information can be obtained from: College Board ATP (Admissions Testing Program), P.O. Box 6200, Princeton, N.J. 08541-6200.

There are also some very simple ways to prepare for cross-cultural entry. During the senior year in high school there could be once-a-week gatherings at which young people and their advisors consider a variety of topics.

A packet for help on cross-cultural entry could be prepared by a school or a mission to be used by a group or by isolated families. The packet could even be sent a unit at a time for use by families during the year prior to returning to the home country.

Suggestions:

1. Plan to have once-a-week gatherings of high school students and advisors.

2. Make up a packet of helpful cross-cultural entry material.

A cross-cultural packet could contain:
1. Stories about families that moved to another culture.
2. Information sheets on the country to which the young person is going, including: (a) climate and clothing; (b) common expressions; (c) sports or other current activities; (d) names in the news; (e) banking and currency to be used; (f) how to find a job; (g) colleges and financial aid; (h) how to study; (i) safety; (j) current popular music; (k) how to find a church and a Bible study and prayer group.
3. A map of the country to which the young person is going, and information on the general geography and history of that country.
4. Work sheets on how to improve communication.
5. A bibliography that will help the young person handle the transition better, and books with which most of her or his peers would be familiar.
6. Videos to help the young person to understand the new environment.
7. One- or two-page articles by those knowledgeable in certain fields could be gathered into a packet. Topics could include preparation for: (a) crucial decisions about sex and drugs; (b) making a budget and handling money; (c) handling a crisis: finding information and help; (d) good relationships with those of the opposite sex; (e) how to use leadership skills in the new setting; (f) handling loneliness, fear, depression, anger, etc.

Each of these suggestions could be the topic discussed at one or more gatherings with the young people who are preparing to go to another culture. The topics in this book could also be used this way.

Financial Aid

There are three major sources of financial aid for college students:
1. From colleges. Get Financial Aid Forms (FAF) from colleges with whom you correspond. This will give you access to their endowments.

2. From the College Scholarship Service, P.O. Box 6300, Princeton, N.J. 08541-6300. This will give you access to government grants.
3. From publications in libraries and university centers describing grants from other than schools and government. These private-sector funds come from businesses, clubs, foundations, etc. The publications will describe for whom the grants are intended and how to apply for them.

Some things to remember:
1. Application forms are available from colleges or the College Scholarship Service.
2. Schools consider financial aid applications six to eight months prior to the school year to which it will be applied.
3. A copy of the parents' most recent U.S. income tax return will be required.
4. Filing early (February) will help you meet application deadlines.

If possible, during furlough establish residence in the state where your MK will be going to college, so that state grants and scholarships will be available.

MKs Say

Give adequate family discussion time to those statements which seem applicable to your situation. Make sure everyone is heard. Take notes; make plans.

MKs say to parents and missions:
✔ *"I needed more vocabulary; better English."*

✔ *"Evaluate home-schooling material, watching for gaps in the education. Teach U.S. geography. Provide good reading material in a variety of areas."*

✔ *"Music, sports, science, etc. should be included. Select high school by correspondence as a last resort. If it is a must, combine with local school for some of the above, as well as the social aspect."*

✔ *"Seek temporary teachers to help in home schooling."*

✔ *"Schooling should not be oppressive or militant."*

✔ *"American school is helpful for high schoolers and can be a preparation for reentry and college. A course on adjusting could be offered."*

✔ *"One year at a good prep school in the U.S. can be helpful."*

MKs say to MKs:

- ✔ *"Apply yourself to your studies; keep studies a priority."*
- ✔ *"Be realistic about course planning and college responsibilities. Get help when needed."*
- ✔ *"Learn to communicate well verbally and in writing."*
- ✔ *"Spend your first several years at a small Christian college."*
- ✔ *"Look for an accredited four-year college, Christian or secular."*
- ✔ *"Go to a public college or university."*

Decision Making

Some of the most emphasized responses from MKs come under decision making, choices and responsibility, including moral values about sex, drugs and alcohol.

Young people living overseas are often in closed communities in which most people think alike. General decisions are made by the group (such as what clothes are acceptable) and most other choices are dictated by parents or the situation (such as saving my allowance because there is no store in which to spend it).

At a secular college young people from Christian homes expect behavior very different from the standards with which they grew up. At a Christian college they can be caught unawares, and do things that aren't the best because they were not prepared; they didn't expect it in that setting.

Like any other human skill, decision making takes practice, and practice means that some decisions will be right and others won't work at all. Both results will contribute toward a young person's learning to make competent decisions. All children need to start practicing decision making early. For MKs, it is crucial that they be equipped to make a majority of sound decisions by the time they enter another culture. They did not spend their childhood years in their parents' home country and, therefore, do not have automatic responses to that culture. In addition, the world has changed drastically since their parents' youth, and the family has not been there to see this change. These facts, taken together with adolescent transition and learning to live on their own, can create havoc in the lives of MKs who do not have an adequate grasp of how to reach solid decisions. Sending an MK off with the self-confidence of knowing how to make wise decisions will equip the young person well for handling the new life.

MKs say they would like to have known:

- ✔ *"About drugs."*

- ✔ *"About the freedom and easy access to drugs, alcohol, and sex."*

- ✔ *"That not all Americans have Christian values, and what non-Christians are like."*

- ✔ *"The values of American youth."*

- ✔ *"More about the U.S. church; what is acceptable, like drinking and dancing, etc."*

- ✔ *"Why I was going to college."*

"Don't turn to chemical outlets."

Decision-Making Process

MKs:

1. List your long-range goals. For example, to become a teacher; to live overseas, etc.
2. Identify your values and number them to show how important each one is to you. For example: honesty, sharing with others, independence, learning, etc.
3. Determine what needs to be decided. For example, what college to choose.
4. Gather information. For example, what colleges have the major you want? What colleges are near people you know? What colleges might give you a scholarship?
5. Think of all the possible actions you could take. For example, choose the college that has the major you want but would cost more. Or, choose the same college as your friend.
6. Consider the possible consequences of each choice—all the pros and cons. Are you deciding for the right reasons?
7. Make a choice.
8. Take action.
9. Be ready to take responsibility for your decision.
10. Evaluate your decision. If you are unhappy with the results of your decision, consider making a new choice or making the best of your original decision.

Good decision making takes good preparation. If your MK is going to college, does she or he know why your family considers this important? Use the advice from other MKs as a starting point for helping your MKs to handle life.

MKs Say

Give adequate family discussion time to those statements that seem applicable to your situation. Make sure everyone is heard. Take notes; make plans.

MKs say to MKs:

✔ *"Develop emotional independence before you leave home (through extra-curricular activities, etc.)."*

✔ *"Learn to be in control of yourself; have plans for what you will do—job, school, etc.; make sure that what you are doing is what you want to do; don't blame others for your problems; learn how to shop."*

✔ *"Don't conform to be accepted—don't change your personality or sacrifice moral values to fit in; choose your friends carefully."*

✔ *"Set standards, make sure your values are right and don't get caught in recent trends."*

✔ *"Respect others' life choices without judging."*

✔ *"There are much more efficient and constructive outlets to your problems than the superficial help from drugs."*

✔ *"Don't jump into marriage, thinking it will take care of your homesickness."*

✔ *"Even in a Christian college expect to find some use of drugs, loose morals, double standards, and legalists."*

"At last I have a job!"

MKs say to parents and missions:

✔ *"Have your priorities in order: God, family, vocation."*

✔ *"Parents need to 'let go'—let kids be responsible and manage their own affairs as early as possible."*

✔ *"Don't be too restrictive and fundamental—don't isolate kids from the real world."*

✔ *"Give practical training: financial preparation, budgeting money, life management, cooking, input into school decisions, preparation for the job market and the secular world."*

Financial Management

One of the major gaps between MKs and their peers is job experience. (See "Work" in Chapter 4.) Being able to handle money wisely and easily is a great asset to an entering MK. Even though a child naturally picks up his or her parents' ways in the use of money, the details of making a budget, making a checkbook balance, and even handling a different currency need to be taught and practiced. Having some coins and paper money with which to practice helps a great deal. An early allowance teaches a youngster something about spending and saving. Parents need to make sure they don't keep adding "extras" to the stipulated amount and that they don't overly influence its use.

Suggestions:

Skills for later dividends
1. Library experience.
2. Computer experience.
3. Experience with audio-visual equipment.
4. Bilingual ability for translation and/or international telephone operator job.
5. Tutoring experience in English, sciences, etc.
6. Typing.
7. Yard work.
8. House cleaning.
9. Baby-sitting.

Handling money
1. An allowance can be a great teacher.
2. Help MKs become familiar with currency of your home country.
3. Practice details of preparing a budget.
4. Practice making a checkbook balance.

A young person who learns to foresee expenses that will fit income will have a practical skill, useful for life. One MK reported that when he went to prep school his dad gave him a check that would cover all of the year's tuition, room and board, books and supplies, clothes, travel, and some extras. The MK put that check in the bank and used the money as it was needed. Both the MK and his parents were delighted when at the end of the year all expenses had been met. That kind of arrangement takes preparation, teaching, and trust.

A family going back to the home country needs to also plan financially. One family made a budget for the months in the U.S., but did not count on the money needed for gifts their many children would be expected to take to birthday parties.

A returning teen MK will always need a little extra pocket money. Years earlier, a family can help the children acquire skills, such as typing or using a computer, that will earn them some money when needed. In college, being an on-call bilingual phone operator can earn you money while studying in your room. Typing papers for others can also be a lucrative business, especially on a word processor. Cleaning in homes, baby-sitting, or yard work can do the same; but a young person needs to know how to do these things.

Credit Cards

Instead of paying cash, many services are available by showing a credit card and signing a receipt, or giving the credit card number over the phone. VISA and Mastercard are issued by many banks, and are widely accepted for business transactions. This is not free money. Monthly bills are mailed to the card-holder, and must be paid.

A young person needs to be taught to handle credit cards (as well as managing bank cards, bank accounts, finances, etc.), and to acquire the basics of keeping a balanced budget before developing a taste for the apparent ease of credit cards. Plan to pay off the entire credit card bill by the due date to avoid high interest charges. Plastic money—credit cards —will open a whole new world for an MK fresh from the mission field. Credit cards can be a timely help, but they can also be the way to a vicious cycle of overspending.

Keep in mind that a single major credit card is usually enough. Take care of the card as if it were actual money, which it is. Never give a credit card number on the phone unless you originated the call. Report a loss promptly (have the phone number and credit card number in some other place than the wallet). The monthly balance should be promptly paid in full, in which case there is usually no interest charge. Finance charges can mount rapidly if the entire balance is not paid. Don't use it for long-term loans (student loans are much cheaper). Don't use it for cash advances (use a bank card for cash). Shop around for the best value. Different banks offer varying rates, fees, and services. Find the one that suits your needs.

If credit is denied there are alternatives: apply to another bank; get a parent to co-sign the application (while they are still around); get a card that is guaranteed by money in a savings account; establish credit by first getting an easier card from a department store or gas company; review file of credit agency for errors (how to do this will be explained if credit is denied).

CREDIT CARDS

Pros: Convenience
Expense records
Buy airline tickets
Use in emergencies
Allow phone orders
Rent videos
Establish credit rating
Serve as identification

Cons: Can be addictive
Contain hidden expenses
Encourage overspending
Can cost more than you think

—If a credit card is too much temptation to overspend, destroy it.—

In vain you rise early and stay up late, toiling for food to eat —
for while they sleep He provides for those He loves.
—*Psa. 127:2.*

The most significant lesson on money is the importance given to it by the family. This will permanently influence the children's value system and, to a great degree, determine their priorities. "We can't afford that" is a very destructive phrase that can hurt MKs. Since we say we live by God's grace, the phrase makes God seem stingy with us. A better response might be "We don't have that in our budget now, but let's pray about it and see what happens." Don't demand, but be sure to ask God to show you if this is his will.

**Encourage your children to go to God with their requests.
And remember to thank him!**

MKs Say

Give adequate family discussion time to those statements that seem applicable to your situation. Make sure everyone is heard. Take notes; make plans.

MKs say they would like to have known:

✔ *"The importance of summer-job experience in order to be more aware of the world of work and gain experience in money management."*

✔ *"How to manage a checking account; the value of the dollar."*

✔ *"More on career planning and the range of career opportunities; the marketability of various jobs."*

✔ *"About available financial aid and sports scholarships."*

MKs say to Mks:

✔ *"Get job experience. Look for a part-time job during high school."*

"Don't expect MKs to be perfect."

Expectations

Expectations color much of what we do and how we see the world. If we expect brown beans to be salty, Boston baked beans taste mighty strange. If we think someone expects us not to make a mistake, we could be petrified by the fear of letting that person down.

MKs often have a special burden to carry. Either their parents expect perfection from them, or they think their parents, extended family, and church look to them as a holy model. In an MK's mind, this could be extended to become what God demands, and, not being able to live up to such a standard, some MKs crash. Adults would do well to monitor not only their language, but, more importantly, what they convey without words in day-to-day living.

On the whole, high expectations and a focus solely toward Christian leadership surround MKs. They are often pushed rather than encouraged, without the adults ever realizing what they are doing. Sharing expectations, and keeping them realistic, helps family members support each other. In order for expectations to be more on target, try the suggestions.

Suggestions:

Sharing expectations

Parents and teens could write out how each would finish these sentences. Then in a sharing time, the family could talk about how each sees this issue.

Teens:

My parents expect me to...

God expects me to...

I expect my parents to...

When I leave home I expect to...

As an adult I expect to...

Parents:

My children expect me to...

God expects me to...

I expect my children to...

When my children leave home I expect to...

When things are not as I expect them to be, I will...

MKs Say

Give adequate family discussion time to those statements that seem applicable to your situation. Make sure everyone is heard. Take notes; make plans.

MKs say to parents and missions:

✔ *"Don't expect MKs to be perfect—accept the humanity in humans."*

✔ *"Don't be surprised that there will have to be adjustments. Expect them."*

MKs say to MKs:

✔ *"Don't expect the U.S. to be like your host country. You will feel like a foreigner. Expect differences, hardship, frustration, embarrassment and fear. Sometimes the shock can come from little unexpected things."*

✔ *"Give yourself at least one year to feel comfortable and more than that to fit in."*

✔ *"Be realistic about your host country in both the good and the bad."*

✔ *"Accept the fact that non-MKs will not totally understand you."*

✔ *"Prepare for worldliness and a materialistic, nominally-Christian society."*

Crisis Handling

With all of these new factors to deal with, some MKs are bound to need help handling a crisis. What does a young person do when sick and far away from home? Learning not to get overwhelmed but to think clearly and find a person who can get the proper help is a handy key in tight situations.

Some missions have toll-free 1-800 phone numbers that MKs can use in emergencies and most missions encourage MKs needing help to call collect to the mission offices.

24-HOUR EMERGENCY NUMBERS IN THE U.S.

Poison information: 1-800-922-1117.

Rape: Check local list, or phone 1 (213) 333-RAPE (long-distance charge).

Suicide prevention: 1-800-944-4690.

In any emergency you may dial "O" (Operator). Stay on line. If you cannot stay on line, give the operator the street address and community where help is needed.

Overcomer's Outreach, 2290 W. Whittier Blvd., Suite D, La Habra, Calif. 90631. A Christian recovery ministry addressing addictions and compulsions. (See p. 131 for more suggestions.)

What to do

■ **When sick.** Check with school or work health clinic.

■ **When out of money.** Call your parents or their mission headquarters.

■ **When not doing well in your studies.** Talk to your academic counselor; drop some extra-curricular activities; find a study companion.

■ **When very discouraged.** Find a friend you can talk to; go see a counselor; let your parents know how you feel.

■ **When offered drugs or alcohol.**
  1. Just say No.
  2. If your No does not settle the question, walk away or leave.
  3. Choose companions carefully.

4. Don't hang out with the crowd that uses them.
5. Check out ahead the entertainment planned for an evening or a party.
6. Don't act superior or preach at others.
7. You can choose a moment alone with a friend to express your feelings about the danger of alcohol and drugs.

■ **When on a date with someone pushing to have sex.**
Prevention:
1. Avoid being alone in a room with someone of the opposite sex.
2. Go out in groups until you know someone well.
3. Avoid lonely, dark places.
4. Set clear standards at the beginning of a relationship, and don't test your limits. (See suggestions on page 96 for what you can say.)
5. Always have money in your pocket for a phone call or a bus or taxi home.
6. Leave and head for where there are other people.

MKs are often more conservative than their counterparts in the parents' home countries. In a class discussion, a college student found that she was the only one against abortion. Another MK stood up against homosexuality and discovered that the kind student that gave her a ride every day was gay. These topics need to be discussed in missionary homes with teenage children.

Sensitive topics such as abortion and homosexuality need to be discussed with your teenagers before they leave home. If you don't know the facts on these issues in today's world, learn them!

Helpful ministry in the area of homosexuality:
Exodus International North America, P.O. Box 2121,
San Rafael, Calif. 94912-2121

■ **When you have lost your baggage or documents**
1. Check immediately with employees of your plane or bus.
2. Make sure that you ALWAYS get a stub for any checked baggage. You need proof that you handed over any item to a carrier.
3. Put your address on the INSIDE of suitcases and packages, as well as outside.
4. Documents are sometimes stolen to be illegally used by others.

Report missing documents immediately to the nearest authority. Never put documents in checked baggage. Never leave documents unattended. Never hand them over to a stranger. A document belt, similar to a money belt, is extra safety. Always put everything away, including money, before you leave a counter.

■ **When the dorm is closing for the holidays and you have nowhere to go**
1. Let friends at the church you are attending, your roommate, and classmates know you need a place to stay.
2. Phone relatives who might invite you to their home.
3. Call your parent's mission board and tell them you need a place to stay. Sometimes they have a list of homes in your area that would welcome you.
4. Keep emergency telephone numbers handy: (a) a relative; (b) mission board office; (c) pastor; (d) school health service; (e) friend from your church; (f) school counselor.

MKs themselves, plus a lot of excellent research, have made us more aware of what helps and what does not help a young person who moves to the parents' home country. Each one is unique, and MKs go to a wide variety of situations. I hope the ideas in these two chapters on family preparation will encourage families to start preparing for cross-cultural entry a long time before it actually happens.

Questions For Reflection

These questions can be used to help parents apply some of the material in the chapter to their own situation.

1. How could such extras as music, art, sports, and home economics be taught overseas in a small MK school situation? In an isolated family situation?

2. What could be meant by "oppressive and militant" schooling?

3. What are some options for a missionary family to be able to afford an overseas international school, or even a prep school in the home country?

4. How can far-away parents encourage an MK in his or her studies?

5. What kinds of activities help children enjoy words?

6. While still encouraging an MK to be an active part of the host culture, how do parents and teachers make sure that the MK has a good grasp of the English language, or the parents' native tongue?

7. What topics would you include in weekly high school cross-cultural entry preparation sessions?

8. What are some of the earliest decisions a small child can begin to make?

9. Are there decisions that high schoolers should not be allowed to make? If yes, what are they?

10. Name 10 facts about drug abuse; alcohol abuse.

11. Explain to an 18-year-old why you don't think premarital sex is a good idea.

12. Why should (or shouldn't) a young person go to college?

13. What kinds of day-to-day activities teach a child not to judge others?

14. Name three instances that depict parents who have not "let go" of their children; three in which the parents have "let go;" three in which parents might confuse "letting go" with poor parenting.

15. What are some ways parents can isolate their children from the world? Mark each answer as a "positive" or "negative" action.

16. List some possible ways MKs can get job experience that is similar to that in the parents' home culture.

17. Name three instances that could lead an MK to think she or he must be perfect.

18. Where could your MK look for help in a crisis?

Work Sheets

Do these work sheets to help you think about the issues raised in Chapter 2.

What are some of the gaps in MK education abroad that you have noticed? Explain.

_____

_____

_____

What do you think a cross-cultural packet should include?

_____

_____

_____

How does a family living in a small interior town teach their children how to shop, ride a bus or subway, and other city activities?

_____

_____

_____

How does a young person develop emotional independence?

_____

_____

_____

How does a person learn to choose good friends?

_____

_____

_____

What is an "adequate" allowance?

_____

_____

_____

What is the responsibility of your mission board toward your children?

_____

_____

_____

Exercise 1: WORD

Instructions: Answer each of the following questions with a word or short phrase that uses the appropriate letter (placed anywhere) from the word PREPARATION below. Many answers are possible.

1. What benefit, to an MK, does a large university offer?
2. What benefit does a small college offer?
3. What is a characteristic, that you perceive, of a child who is not a "word" person (i.e., one skilled in vocabulary, writing, speaking)?
4. Name an automatic response in your host society.
5. Name an automatic response in your home country society.
6. What prepares a young person well for choosing a life's mate and getting married?

7. What is a family activity that could teach a child the value of a dollar/pound/mark?
8. What is one way a family could learn what financial aid is available for college?
9. Name a Bible chapter (verse if possible) that is a basis for your position on dancing.
10. What should an MK who is far from home do when sick?
11. Where could your MK look for help in a crisis?

1. _____ P

2. _____ R

3. _____ E

4. _____ P

5. _____ A

6. _____ R

7. _____ A

8. _____ T

9. _____ I

10. _____ O

11. _____ N

Exercise 2: TAKE 5

What are five options for a missionary family to be able to afford an international school, or even a prep school in the home country?

_____

_____

_____

_____

_____

Name five ways faraway parents can encourage an MK in her or his studies.

_____

_____

_____

_____

_____

Name five activities to help children enjoy words.

_____

_____

_____

_____

_____

Give five ways parents and teachers can make sure that MKs have a real grasp of the English (or your native tongue) language, while still encouraging them to actively participate in the host culture.

_____

_____

_____

_____

_____

List five topics you would include in weekly high school cross-cultural prep sessions.

_____

_____

_____

_____

_____

What are five decisions a small child can begin to make?

_____

_____

_____

_____

_____

List five facts about drug abuse: Five about alcohol abuse:

_____   _____

_____   _____

_____   _____

_____   _____

_____   _____

List five ways parents can isolate their kids from the world. Mark each answer as a "positive" or "negative" action, as you see it.

_____

_____

_____

_____

_____

Give five reasons a person should (or shouldn't) go to college.

_____

_____

_____

_____

_____

Name five day-to-day activities that teach a child not to judge others.

_____

_____

_____

_____

_____

List five ways an MK can obtain job experience similar to that in your home country.

_____

_____

_____

_____

_____

Exercise 3: SCENARIO

Instructions: Your family could act out these skits, the children playing the role of the adults and vice versa. You will probably be amazed at some of your children's statements. Keep listening!

1. You live overseas in a small rural community. Your four children go to the MK schoolhouse with four other children, eight total. How would you advise the teacher to provide extras such as music, art, sports, and home economics?

2. You have just received a letter from your child who is 2,000 miles away at a boarding school. It reads, "Dear Mom and Dad, Please let me come home. I hate it here. It is so oppressive; everything is militant style..." Your two older children spent four years at the same place and loved it. What, then, would you perceive "oppressive and militant" to mean?

3. Your child just turned 15. She or he is pulling at the reins, wanting more independence. Are there decisions she or he should not be allowed to make? Which ones? Why?

4. You go on furlough and the first thing you do is visit your 18-year-old who has been in college for six months. He is considering sharing an apartment with his girlfriend. How do you explain to him why you don't think free sex is an option?

Now you write the scenario. Describe an instance that depicts the following situations:

1. Parents who have not "let go."

2. Parents who have "let go."

3. Parents who might confuse "letting go" with poor parenting.

4. An MK led to believe she or he must be perfect.

3

Self-Identity

Stress can be stimulating. The key is control. As long as we feel we have some control over the situation, we can adjust in healthy ways.

—Shirley Torstrick

I had just returned to the United States for college. I was excited and scared all at once.

Everyone seems to be in a hurry and to know where they are going, I thought. I don't think I'll ever catch on.

I lived through registration, even getting one or two of the classes I really wanted. One secretary actually smiled at me and showed me how to complete my form.

Back in the dorm that evening, all the girls on my hall gathered for a party. Pictures of important people had been tacked on the wall for each one to identify. I had no idea who the man with the tall red-white-and-blue hat and pointed, white beard could be.

As we checked our lists at the end of the game, the other girls noticed the blank on my paper.

"Alma," they exclaimed, "don't you know Uncle Sam? Every American knows Uncle Sam!"

I quickly crushed my paper and smiled weakly.

I don't have any Uncle Sam, I thought. Besides, why such a big fuss about one uncle anyway? I'm just as American as they are. I even have a passport to prove it.

This young American citizen has lived abroad most of her life and is now entering her parents' home country. Most MKs don't have serious academic problems. Their difficulties are in social adjustment. They are confused about their self-identity, partly because they have always heard how wonderful this "homeland" is. Yet very little seems to be going right for the new arrivals. The money seems strange, their peers have other agendas, the conversations around them seem to be in code, and even for a game like Trivial Pursuit, they have information that doesn't seem to fit the questions. Adjustment usually comes eventually, but is it a good adjustment, or does it leave a residue of pain?

Positive Preparation

For younger MKs entering, frequently for a limited period of time, there are also personal identity problems. They are often over-exposed to the public, feeling ill at ease, and unsure about how to respond. They feel like they are not persons, but MKs, a curiosity, and parents need to remember that the children will need an extra portion of love and understanding, liberally sprinkled with humor. Learning to laugh together can be a valuable escape valve as well as enriching life for all.

Often a parent needs to be away a lot, both on the mission field and during itineration in the home country. Explaining to the kids about how God is using the parent for an important job could be helpful. A missionary family in such a situation tells this:

"Twelve years later our kids met half a dozen missionaries who had been 'called' on that parent's trip. They were deeply happy to realize that they had contributed to such a harvest. They felt like a real part of the team."

Suggestions for kids during itineration or deputation
Small Children
1. Take along place mats so that they eat at the "same" place each time.
2. Evening routine. Keep the same sequence as much as possible. If hosts eat late, feed the kids at a restaurant like McDonald's and put them to bed first.
3. Use one toy bag for car; another when you stop and overnight.

All Children
1. Time and room to roam. Build in recreation and fun time. Stop in state parks or at playgrounds.
2. Accept feelings. "I understand" sincerely said makes a hard job easier.
3. Use the library and road maps. Learn about a new area with your children. Look for interesting spots along your route.

4. New (to the child) Sunday schools are often very difficult for an MK because he or she does not belong with the other children. One parent might lead a family Sunday school and then take the children to the church service where the children are relatively inconspicuous. This keeps the MK from being put on the spot.
5. There will be times when a parent needs to stay home with the children so that they have some continuity in studies and church life.
6. A word of caution as you relate to your supporting churches: Be honest in what you say as you describe your work on the mission field, and in what you write in prayer letters. Great harm is done to your children when they know you have added to the truth to make an interesting story.

Suggestions:

Remember: Traveling to visit churches in the homeland can be very disruptive to family life.

Some possible helps:
1. Include the children in some of your planning. They could contribute a poster about your mission work, or a two-minute taped message about their life on the mission field, for you to play for the Sunday school in the churches you are visiting.

2. Explain to the children how God is using all of you for an important job.

3. Set aside occasional weekends to be with your family. These could center on significant events such as birthdays, or for special happenings such as an important school game. Do not allow other requests to cancel these plans.

4. Sometimes the husband could stay home with the kids, and the wife could take the speaking engagement.

The Child in The Family

One MK said, "When I was twelve, I became involved in dad's work. He was a minister with a large mission field and his including me helped me decide I wanted to do that, too. I enjoyed driving, which he let me do on the deserted dirt roads, and often he would talk to me, pointing out the difference we could both see in a man before and after accepting Christ."

This same MK described Sunday morning in his home when his parents would say happily, "Time to go to church now." He ascribes his positive feelings about himself to this early joyful and accepting attitude of his parents. In fact, the key positive influence on MKs is contented and loving parents.

"How do I pay for this?"

The Child as an Individual

Before "finding their niche," many MKs sense a loss of status upon leaving the host environment overseas, and a common defense is to act "holier" than their peers. However, as long as an MK feels above or better than peers, the adjustment will be hindered. A point to remember might be the fact that Jesus took part in the church and community during his days on earth, certainly an environment different from his usual one.

MKs on the mission field are often leaders in their school, church, and social environment. They have the richness of two cultures to draw upon for resources and often they naturally imitate their parents' roles. Upon returning to their parents' homeland they find themselves at a disadvantage in their peer group, having to learn many of the basics of relating to others in this new context. Parents and mentors can encourage the MK to take leadership in small groups such as InterVarsity or Intramurals, thus helping the MK to repair his or her self image of one who is able to contribute to the group.

Being different, or unique, can also be an advantage, for the person has something special to add to the situation.

MKs Say

Give adequate family discussion time to those statements which seem applicable to your situation. Make sure everyone is heard. Take notes; make plans.

MKs say they would like to have known:

✔ *"Americans thought that I was different and I would feel like an outsider."*

✔ *"I would feel a loss of identity and need help in dealing with this and establishing my identity again."*

✔ *"I needed a more realistic view of myself, not considering myself a hero."*

✔ *"In Brazil we were better off than most, but in the U.S. we were poor."*

MKs say to MKs:

✔ *"Don't be embarrassed about your background or shy about letting people know you are from another country (they expect those that look American to act American). Count yourself lucky to have experienced your past."*

✔ *"Preserve your uniqueness—be realistic, others will see you as different."*

✔ *"Be honest with yourself; learn about yourself—goals, priorities, weaknesses, strengths. Take tests—career aptitude and personality inventories."*

MKs say to parents and missions:

✔ *"Parents, let kids know they are the number one priority."*

✔ *"Mission leaders, make qualified Christian counseling available during college years."*

"Let kids know they are number one priority."

The drama of cross-cultural entry brings on a new evaluation of the self-image. Help can be found for the MK in these areas:

1. **Learning who she or he is.** An MK's sense of self-worth can be reinforced by an invitation from other young people to become a part of the youth group.

2. **Learning to adjust to the new environment.** An MK can look around for a young person who knows what is "in" in clothes and ask for help in adapting his or her wardrobe.

3. **Having adequate support systems that provide the needed kinds of assistance.** A nearby adult who understands the MK's needs, or a friend who can teach the MK such things as how to work the microwave in the cafeteria.

4. **Maintaining some family traditions.** At college, finding some friend who will enjoy sharing a Saturday morning pancake breakfast, even if at the cafeteria.

Even though a person changes to a new culture, not everything about that person will change. An MK needs to know that she or he will continue being the same person in the new setting. Talking about what changes and what does not will help the family members better visualize the new situation and to feel more secure. Things like love of music, interest in books, and a desire to be outdoors will continue, even though the expression of these things will adapt to the new location. The MK can learn to ice skate rather than swim, and country music might be highlighted over Latin rhythms.

This stays the same		This changes	
This is me		*In host country*	*In parent's home country*
Love of music	→	Latin rhythms	←→ Country music
Interest in books	→	A few at home	←→ Libraries full
Desire to be outdoors	→	Swim	←→ Ice skate
Like to help people	→	Teach a Good News Club	←→ Tutor a foreign student

Facing Separation

MKs don't "go home" when they grow up. They leave home. Loneliness is a feeling common to MKs who have recently entered a new culture. An MK is like someone who knows a secret and must keep it, having to submerge the overseas experience because few are interested. It seems that no one listens or really cares. Feeling lonely, however, is universal, and it helps to realize this. It is said that TCKs (Trans-Cultural Kids) support the post office, phone company, and airlines because relationships are important to them. The following quotes speak to this.

MKs Say

Give adequate family discussion time to those statements which seem applicable to your situation. Make sure everyone is heard. Take notes; make plans.

MKs say they would like to have known:

✔ *"How much I would miss the Brazilian flag, music, etc. I wish someone had encouraged me to bring some of those things to college."*

✔ *"That Americans would seem superficial and cold; that relatives didn't really want me; that most people are only interested in their own world."*

✔ *"That other MKs could really help me as a support group."*

✔ *"Not to negatively compare the two countries."*

✔ *"That it is OK to call home more than once a year."*

MKs say to MKs:

✔ *"It helps to return to a familiar area (geographic), and locate near relatives."*

✔ *"Keep busy."*

MKs say to parents:

✔ *"Phone college students monthly."*

✔ *"Make an effort to see your children at least once a year."*

Loneliness becomes most dangerous during the year after college or other formal studies, if the MK is not married. The sadness and grief over separations is sometimes still unresolved and is more intense when the grief is: (a) multiple; (b) simultaneous; (c) intense; (d) unresolved; (e) borne alone.

The grief pattern generally follows the five known stages of denial, anger, bargaining, depression, and finally acceptance of the situation, even though some of the stages might be so short as not to be very noticeable. Being able to acknowledge the grief and be helped through the sequence is a healing process.

**TO ACKNOWLEDGE GRIEF
+ ACCEPT HELP THROUGH IT = HEALING**

Helping The Child Grieve
Over Separations

It is important for parents and child to talk it out so that the MK knows parents care. This also lets MKs know that it's all right for them to go on with their life without feeling guilty.

Someone needs to be there in the new setting (such as a boarding school) to help the child grieve over separations. The child needs to know that it is all right to feel sad, and that someone understands how she or he feels.

"TCKs need to be encouraged to resolve relationships by saying good-by to people and places. They need to mourn endings to be able to celebrate new beginnings" (Alice Brawand).

Facing the reality of a good-by and helping each other over the hurt is much healthier than pretending no one cares.

Many mission boards provide at least one round-trip home during the college years for the MK to visit parents on the mission field. This policy pays high dividends in the emotional health of both MK and missionary parents.

Saying Good-by

Help MKs say good-by to people and places by:
1. Talking with the family about a prospective move.
    (a) Younger children: a few weeks before moving.
    (b) School-age children: as soon as plans are definite.
2. Listening to the children talk about their sadness at leaving friends.
3. Visiting the people and places the MK will miss, and making a little ceremony of leave-taking, such as taking a picture, giving a special gift, saying a prayer, etc.

4. Taking with you mementos that are meaningful to the MK, such as a picture of a pet, marbles played with a buddy, a smooth stone from the fishing hole.
5. Assuring the MK that she or he can phone and write and maybe someday even visit this home place again.
6. Talking with the family about some of the things of interest to them in the new home.

Reading this book will often bring back experiences and feelings of loneliness to adult MKs. Recognizing these can be a step in resolving hurts that have been carried along for many years.

Depression And Suicide

Normal depression can come with the hard knocks in life, or even due to a change of body hormones. Usually it does not last long, and is not a deep rejection of life. However, depressive illness is a serious malfunction of the body which needs medical help, and which often is a precursor of suicide attempts. The National Center for Health Statistics in 1984 revealed that suicide, for the first time in U.S. history, moved from third to second place (behind accidents) as the leading cause of death for 15-to-24-year-olds.[1] Today's statistics still show suicide as the second greatest cause of death among American young people.

A person with low self-image is more likely to commit suicide. These individuals do not like themselves and find it difficult to believe others care about them. For a self-perceived "worthless" individual, dying seems preferable to living. Or, a suicide attempt may be a drastic plea for help.

Jesus said, "I am the light of the world.
Whoever follows me will never walk in darkness,
but will have the light of life" (John 8:12).

"Be strong and courageous. Do not be afraid or
terrified because of them (your enemies,) for the
Lord your God goes with you; he will never leave
you nor forsake you" (Deut. 31:6).

One of the contributing factors in this desperate situation is the frightening world in which we live. Young people are asking, "Will there be a world to live in when I'm 30?" Violent crime, terrorist bombings, a nuclear accident or war, the breakdown of the ozone layer, products laced with cyanide all remind us that we basically have no control over our environment. Fear and anxiety are the results. The only way to peace is in trusting God's promises. Jesus is the Light in this dark world, and if we follow him, we will not only become part of the world's hope, but we will also not be terrified by fear.

Teen and young adult MKs are not exempt from the statistics on suicide. They do have the help of coming from homes where faith is an important ingredient, and many become integrated into the extended family of the church. On the negative side, however, they can feel deeply isolated and not know how to ask for help. Added to this are feelings of not wanting to bother parents who are "sacrificing" to serve the Lord. To a confused mind, dying can even mean not ever having to move again. It can be thought of as staying in one place for the rest of life.

HOW TO RECOGNIZE DEPRESSIVE ILLNESS

1. Recurrent thoughts of death and suicide.
2. Feelings of hopelessness.
3. Neglect of personal appearance.
4. Trouble concentrating.
5. Change in sleep or appetite patterns.
6. Complaints of physical illness.
7. Can be camouflaged by an overly happy and active exterior.

Medical diagnosis and treatment is the first and most urgent need. Counseling can come later.

What to do

Realize the person who has depressive illness has their thinking and judgment impaired and cannot make sound decisions. Get the person to a doctor who can help. Depressive illness usually responds well to medical treatment.

Preventing suicide is not a complicated social problem. Prevention depends mainly on recognizing the depressive illness that usually comes before a suicide attempt.

TEEN SUICIDE CAN BE PREVENTED

1. **Listen.** An opener could be, "I know you've been through a hard time and wondered if you'd like to talk about it."
2. **Be honest.** If the person's words scare you, say so. If you don't know how to respond, say so.
3. **Share feelings.** Sharing your own down experiences can help the person realize she or he is not alone.
4. **Get help.** It is always better to ask the person directly if she or he is considering suicide. A high risk exists if concrete plans have been made. Look for a local suicide hotline in the phone book, or call Suicide Prevention 1-800-944-4690. Get the troubled person to speak to a physician or minister. (See added information on suicide prevention in Appendix G and H.)

Perhaps the heaviest burden of all for young adult MKs is their perception of the expectations of perfection from both parents and God. This mix of perceptions comes from day-to-day life beginning at very young ages. Parents who serve God on the mission field out of grateful, joyful hearts, rather than as an obligation their God requires, transmit to their children a loving, trustworthy Father. God is not out to inflict pain on them or their children. It is therefore easier to expect God's help during the confusion and hurt of cross-cultural entry.

Most adults realize that only God is perfect. In striving to introduce God to children, parents point at perfection. But often they seem to mean they expect it of themselves and of their children. It has been said that children don't need perfect parents. They need imperfect parents trying faithfully to serve a perfect God.

Stress can be beneficial as long as a person has some feeling of control over life. However, all of these seemingly small factors can add up to the complete desperation that leads to suicide. Most of the warning signs that should alert caring adults are rather common sense. Probably the most misunderstood, and therefore ignored, are statements such as the following by the young person:

> "I want to die."
>
> "I don't want to live any more."
>
> "They'll be sorry when I am gone."

Take seriously statements about killing oneself. If you note other signs of depressive illness, and are concerned, ask whether the teen has thought that she or he would be "better off dead." You will not put the idea in his or her mind. If the teen has planned how she or he might do it, and has the means to carry it out, seek immediate help.

It is a myth that people who talk about suicide don't do it.[2] The fact is that at least eight out of ten suicide victims have spoken about their intent before killing themselves. Another myth is that the person's mind should be diverted from such a topic and the subject of the conversation should be changed. The fact is that the person should be taken seriously, listened to with care, given a chance to express himself or herself and encouraged to find help. Often, fear of the subject and feelings of complete inadequacy make one want to run from sharing such a pain in another's heart. Being alert and caring in crisis situations is enhanced by remembering that suicide is a terrible waste of life and its success is irrevocable.

"Talking and listening and trying to understand MKs of all ages is always a worthwhile use of time. Understanding doesn't mean agreeing. It means only that you hear and know what they are talking about. MKs need to know it is okay to feel angry, or sad, or upset. They need to know that these feelings are perfectly normal for both Christians and non-Christians. MKs and the adults around them also need to realize that often, if they can just be patient, things will get better"(Shirley Torstrick).

Once we learn that children can handle truth if it is presented in a sensitive way, we are freer to admit our mistakes and heartaches on levels that are appropriate for the children's maturity. A college student not doing too well in a course, for instance, can take heart when learning that dad failed a course in college, too.

Share your successes and some of your failures with your kids. Both help the MKs to know that they too are pretty normal human beings, very much like mom and dad.

Child Abuse

One of the key negative influences on any child, MKs included, is child abuse. Even though it should not happen in Christian homes, and certainly not in missionary homes, these are made up of human beings, some of whom either grew up in abusive situations and acquired their pattern, or have found the stresses of life overpowering and take out their frustrations on weaker family members around them. At times missionary life can be lonesome, tiring, and overwhelming, and raising children is a difficult and demanding twenty-four hour a day job. That parents sometimes get angry or impatient is no wonder. But to abuse a child in any way is very serious. How that child sees himself or herself will forever be damaged by physical, emotional, sexual, or any other abuse. If you think you might harm your child, you must look for help. Find a counselor in your area or make a trip to a counselor if there is no one near you. You can also write for help to the ministries listed on this page.

RESOURCES AGAINST CHILD ABUSE

For information about child sexual abuse, contact your local Family and Children Services agency, or call the national office in the USA at 414-359-1040.

"Family Violence" is a 6- to 10-session guide that provides case studies and discussion questions for use by laity and clergy who wish to develop appropriate responses to violence within families. Order from the CWC (Committee of Women of Color) Women's Ministry Unit, 100 Witherspoon St., Louisville, Ky. 40202. Attention Connie Hobbs, room 4611. Phone (502) 569-5380. Please include a check for $6, payable to CWC.

Other helpful sources:

Desert Stream Ministries, c/o Jonathan Hunter, 12488 Venice Blvd., Los Angeles, Calif. 90066-3804.

Parenting, Box 2866P, Chicago, Ill. 60690. Ask for free booklet.

For information about a Child Abuse Ministry Project, contact Bonnie Glass MacDonald, 100 Witherspoon St., Room 3041, Louisville, Ky. 40202-1396. Phone (502) 569-5789.

Faith

Faith is fundamental to personal identity. As parents in full-time Christian service, our deepest yearning is that our children come to understand what it means to accept Christ as their savior, commit their lives to our Lord, and then build the Word of God into their daily lives.

Because children tend to imitate their parents, some of the visible characteristics of Christianity, such as going to church, or "saying your prayers," will take place. But as MKs reach adulthood and independence, they will be bombarded with many claims other than those of Christ, and with many ideas from which they have been sheltered on the mission field.

In order to stand firm in their Christian beliefs, MKs need to have a clear concept of the basics of the Christian faith; they need to know why these beliefs are important; they need to know some of the main arguments against Christianity; they need to know how to use the Bible for worship, for growing as Christians, and for finding answers to the dilemmas of their daily lives today. In other words, they need to be discipled.

It is possible for missionary parents to be good disciplers in what they consider their "work," and fail to follow a carefully laid out plan with their own children.

Some of the training in faith in our homes has to do with our example as parents. Do we treat others, even in the privacy of our home, in loving and kind ways? Much has to do with how our words match our actions. Do we tell the children that Jesus wants them to share, and then give to others only what we no longer need or want?

We also need a plan to present each child with Christ's claims and help that child come to understand and make a decision about his or her faith. Within this plan we need to help the MK learn to use the Bible.

For a teenager, we need to provide helpful material and information so that she or he can include in the Bible study:

1. The meaning of the original text.
2. How this text can be applied today.
3. How other religions might see this text.

Suggestions:

Disciple your MKs
—Teach the basics of the Christian faith.
—Show why these basics are important.
—Share some arguments others will have against Christianity.
—Teach them how to study the Bible.
—Instill in them a habit of memorizing Scripture.
—Demonstrate Christian principles in your life.
—Give them an opportunity for decision.
—Pray with and for your MK, always.

Cults

College campuses and other places where young people gather are prime targets for cults looking for recruits. On the surface, cults can seem like a warm fellowship of committed Christians, but they are absolutely ruthless in their motives and methods. They want to control and use people.

Warning to MKs

Beware of religious groups that:
1. Try to forcibly drag you into their group.
2. Have a leader who claims to be all-knowing and appears wealthy.
3. Expect orders to be obeyed blindly.
4. Are above the law.
5. Require constant fund raising.
6. Sever ties with family and friends.

7. Have world domination as a goal.
8. Restrict free contact with the outside world.
9. Claim to be Christian, but interpret the Bible in their own way.

For your safety, make no commitments until you have checked them out. Ask others on campus about the group. Ask the campus chaplains or your church pastor about the group. (For help, contact Spiritual Counterfeits Project, Box 2418, Berkeley, Calif. 94702. Request their catalog with information on "new religions," or, in an emergency, phone them (415) 527-9212).

MKs Say

Give adequate family discussion time to those statements that seem applicable to your situation. Make sure everyone is heard. Take notes, make plans.

MKs say to MKs:
- ✔ *"Have a strong personal faith and keep your faith in God."*
- ✔ *"Have a regular 'Quiet Time.'"*
- ✔ *"Develop a strong prayer life, asking for wisdom in your decisions."*
- ✔ *"Don't compromise your faith."*
- ✔ *"Find a good church."*

MKs say to parents and missions:
- ✔ *"Pray for kids."*

MKs say to missionary families:
- ✔ *"Spend time with your children."*
- ✔ *"Establish a bond of love, respect and security."*
- ✔ *"Be a model of a biblically structured life."*
- ✔ *"Create an awareness of God in your home through such happenings as Bible study and devotions."*
- ✔ *"Help your children understand your motivation for serving God."*
- ✔ *"Establish a pattern of goal setting."*
- ✔ *"Give your children opportunities for ministry."*
- ✔ *"Pray for your children from the very beginning."*
- ✔ *"Pray with your children as naturally as they speak to you."*

Any parent too busy to pray each day and write each week (after the MK leaves home) is too busy. Passing on our faith is never automatic. It is by God's grace and with much prayer.

A word for Christian parents whose adult children have chosen not to follow Christ: A decision for or against Christ is an individual decision. God has given us this freedom and we must respect our children's freedom, too. Keep on loving and including your MK in the family, and never give up praying that God will work in that life in his own way, in his own time. Ask joyfully and trust completely.

Advantages of Being an MK

An MK's self-image could be pretty low simply because there is so much to learn in dealing with two or more cultures. MKs and their parents need to have clearly in mind the substantial assets of a person raised in more than one culture. When the going gets rough, remembering an MK's strong points can cheer the spirits and give renewed courage.

WHAT MKs DO BEST

1. Versatile in languages.
2. More mature than their peers.
3. Excellent observers.
4. Open to learning.
5. Adapt all over the world.
6. Valuable in multinational situations.
7. See the world in three dimensions.
8. Service oriented.
9. Have had an opportunity to see God at work in special ways.

MKs' strong points

1. **Linguistic ability.** MKs grow up hearing at least two languages. By playing with their new friends on the mission field they naturally learn the second language, most often becoming fluent much quicker than their parents. Their studies are often in two or more languages. This natural training gives MKs a solid basis for acquiring and using languages throughout their lives.

2. **Maturity.** A young MK is often two to three years ahead of monocultural children in school. Many teen and young adult MKs are prepared to handle life's problems in more mature ways than their peers.

3. **Cross-cultural skills.**
   (a) <u>Excellent observer.</u> Because MKs have often crossed cultural barriers, they have learned not to take their environment for granted. Frequent moves have trained them to notice detail in their surroundings and in people with whom they have contact.
   (b) <u>Teachable.</u> An MK knows that there is a lot more to the world than meets anyone's eye at any one time. She or he can also see many points of view, so is more tolerant.
   (c) <u>Is not restricted by geography.</u> Having lived in many places, an MK is usually willing and able to adapt to a variety of settings.
   (d) <u>Valuable to the multinational job market.</u> Much of the orientation to a new location is second nature to an MK.

4. **World view.** To an MK, the world is three-dimensional rather than flat; is experienced first-hand, rather than learned from TV and newspapers.

5. **Service oriented.** If an MK is not helping someone, she or he is likely to feel guilty. The MK has grown up in a ministry setting where helping others is a way of life. The MK needs to realize this and use this commendable bent in wise ways that don't smother another person, or disregard the MK's own needs.

6. **Faith.**
   (a) An MK can have a larger God-view, knowing that God's creation is much more vast than any one culture.
   (b) An MK can have the basics decided, and so be free to handle other things.
   (c) Basics. Do I believe in God? Do I allow Jesus first place in my life? Do I give priority to learning from the Bible?

The challenge is for MKs to "play the game" of cross-cultural entry well, have fun at it and not miss too many plays. That leads to genuine adjustment and a positive self-identity.

End Notes

1. Dave Capuzzi, *Counseling and Intervention Strategies for Adolescent Suicide Prevention* (Ann Arbor, Mich.: University of Michigan, 1988).
2. Ibid.

Questions For Reflection

These questions can be used to help parents apply some of the material in the chapter to their own situation.

1. Name 10 famous people known to college freshmen today.

2. What is the difference between coping and adjusting?

3. What response could your child give when confronted with a Sunday school teacher who says to the class, "Children, Timmy is a real live missionary!"

4. What can parents do, or say to their children, when on occasion the parents do not feel like going to a particular church or service?

5. What suggestions do you have for a missionary family to have some family time during intensive itineration?

6. Why might an MK feel like a hero?

7. Are missionaries rich or poor? Give reasons for your answer.

8. How can parents show their kids that they are number one priority?

9. Name some possible "support systems" for an MK.

10. List five important family traditions. How could your MKs keep them up when they are far away from home?

11. Why can the year after a single MK graduates from college be the most lonesome year?

12. What are some ways a person can say good-by to people and places?

13. What sorts of experiences contribute to our self-image?

14. Give five danger signals that could mean a young person is seriously considering suicide.

15. Describe some ways in which truth can be presented in a sensitive way.

16. Give five steps you would take if a young person said to you, "I want to die."

17. Give some possible topics to be included in our prayers for MKs.

18. How can we help our children have a strong personal faith in Jesus?

Work Sheets

What is the difference between coping and adjusting?

_____

_____

Are missionaries poor or rich? Explain.

_____

_____

How can parents show their children that they are No. 1 priority?

_____

_____

List five of your family traditions. In what ways could your MK continue them when away from home?

_____   _____

_____   _____

_____   _____

_____   _____

_____   _____

Why can the year after a single MK graduates from college be the most lonesome year?

_____

_____

_____

What sorts of experiences contribute to our self-identity?

_____

_____

_____

How can we help our children have a strong personal faith in Jesus?

_____

_____

_____

Exercise 1: WHAT DO YOU SAY, DEAR?

You are an MK itinerating with your parents. You walk in to the 149th Sunday school classroom and the teacher says, "Children, Timmy is a real live missionary!" What do you say?

_____

_____

_____

_____

It is Sunday. Your negative feelings toward attending a particular church service or other obligation are coming through. Your 12-year-old wants an explanation of your feelings. What do you say?

_____

_____

_____

_____

You are a missionary preacher. This Sunday you spoke on loneliness and made the passing remark "loneliness is a symptom." After the service someone comes up to you and asks, "What do you mean by 'loneliness is a symptom'?" What do you say?

_____

_____

_____

_____

A missionary comes to you for advice. He says, "I have moved 37 times over three continents in my life, but I still don't know how to say good-by." What do you say?

_____

_____

_____

_____

How can truth be presented in a sensitive way? When someone asks for
your opinion and it will hurt them, what do you say?

_____

_____

_____

_____

Exercise 2: LISTS, BIG AND LITTLE

Instructions: Read the lists below carefully. Which do you know the
most about? Which do you know the least about? Write down your lists.
How do your lists compare to others doing the exercise? How could you
increase your knowledge about the topic on your shortest list? How
could you share your knowledge about the topic on your longest list?

List famous people known to college freshmen today.

List suggestions for family time during intensive itineration

List reasons why an MK might feel like a hero.

List possible "support systems" for an MK.

List danger signals that could mean a young person is seriously considering suicide.

List steps you would take if a young person said to you, "I want to
die."

List possible topics to be included in your prayers for MKs.

4

Steps to a Successful Transition

Instead of preoccupation about their children being "handicapped" by the overseas experience, missionaries and other overseas parents should focus on the significant advantages of a child who grows up "international."

—Ted Ward

I had lived most of my eighteen years on a mission field frontier. The summer before college I spent with my grandparents who lived on the outskirts of a quiet little town in Ohio. There were many summer chores to do around the place—cleaning out the gutters, painting the back steps, and, of course, yard work. I wasn't afraid of work and was glad to be able to help. A few days after arriving I said I would like to go out and cut the grass.

"Great," said grandfather. "The lawn mower is in the back shed."

I hesitated to tell my grandfather that I had never before used a power lawn mower. Actually, I had only seen one in a catalog. Without asking for help, I got the mower out, and having some idea of how it functioned, got it started and struggled to control its path.

The grass was pretty tall. Soon the motor was choking and, without turning it off, I reached down to pull at the ball of grass. Everything went black. When I came to, I had lost four fingers.

This MK paid a high price for lack of information in the ways of the new culture. Information, culture habits, and how to do things are all second nature to those who grow up in a particular society. They have a lot of time to watch and hear and learn. An 18-year-old MK coming into that society has some pieces of this puzzle, but there are big gaps in the most unexpected places. A boy new to the mission field frontier could get his fingers cut off with big hunting knives, but the MK in the story above knew how to handle a hunting knife. What he didn't know was how to use a power mower safely.

Safety First

In fact, safety should be a major topic in preparing an MK for cross-cultural entry. There are booklets that can be obtained from the United States on safety in all sorts of areas: in the home, in camping, in using power tools, in driving, in bicycling, in preventing fires. Bicycling in the interior of Brazil and in Chicago require vastly different skills, and a young person can be made aware of this before being exposed to new dangers. (For help in teaching safety, send for the Missionary Resource Book, International Aid, 17011 W. Hickory, Spring Lake, Mich. 49456; telephone 616-846-7490).

Speaking of safety, does your MK know how to swim? Knowing how to swim is valuable insurance against falling in water and not being able to get out. Make sure your MK knows how to swim.

In answer to the question, "What would you like to have known before entering your parents' home country," some MKs said:

✔ *"I needed to be better prepared to travel alone and to live alone."*

✔ *"I needed a better understanding of the wide choices of a college, the enrollment process and college activities."*

✔ *"I needed to understand the school penalty system."*

These answers illustrate shocks felt by returning MKs and some of the details parents overlook as they prepare their MKs for living away from home. For instance, parents might automatically enroll their child in the parents' alma mater, leaving the MK with very little hands-on experience of dealing with the school, finding out what steps are needed to get a desired course, or how to become part of a group, such as the chorus or the soccer team.

Some of the MKs' reactions are simply because they have absorbed a different culture and their responses may need to be modified. For instance, a young man going out alone with a young lady means two different things in the United States and in Brazil. In Brazil (until very recently, and even now in many circles) a couple alone means a certain commitment to one another, or that the families are long-time friends. In the States, a date is most often just a way to get to know a person.

Handling Sex

In recent years, the sexual revolution has changed the American scene. Experimenting with sex in all of its forms is not only allowed by society in general but encouraged by educators and leaders. Young people can fall into the trap of using sex to boost low self-esteem or because of a confused identity. Too late, the teenagers find out that it not only doesn't work that way, but instead adds to their problems.

Being important to someone is a basic need. Knowing we are loved by

God for who we are and not for what we do brings us inner security. Then we are free to trust others to love us for ourselves and not for what we do. True and lasting intimacy comes from being able to share thoughts and dreams in heart-to-heart conversations, getting to know and accept each other unconditionally. This accepting love is the yearning of all hearts. Young people need to be warned that casual sex does not produce this fulfilling intimacy. Excellent conversations produce lasting intimacy.

Remember, you never "owe" sex to anyone but your marriage partner. Sexual intercourse outside of marriage rarely leads to your partner loving you more. It often leads to a more casual relationship and to disillusionment. Learn to enjoy your sexuality and the companionship of the opposite sex, but keep intimate physical contact for after marriage. Do not promise by gesture or attitude more than you can give before marriage. Have ready ideas for alternatives to going to bed with your date. Quickly involve other people, if your date is becoming too intimate.

Sexual relationships influence physical health as well as emotional health. Sexually transmitted diseases such as gonorrhea, syphilis, venereal warts, and AIDS are serious health problems in our society and result in a high cost to individuals in suffering, money, and life itself. Some of these diseases are not readily apparent, and can be contracted by an unsuspecting occasional partner. A teen who chooses to wait for sex within marriage almost always can avoid the serious health problems that accompany sexually transmitted diseases. If you suspect a problem, find medical help right away. Your school's health care center, or a public health clinic are two possible options.

Suggestions:

Ways to say No to having sex:
1. "I am just not ready yet."
2. "I care about you, but I don't want the responsibility that comes with sex."
3. "I think sex outside of marriage is wrong."
4. "I feel good about not having sex until I am married. I've made my decision and I feel comfortable with it."
5. "If you cared for me, you wouldn't push."

Teenage MKs returning to their parents' home country need to be prepared in the following areas:

1. Know that many of their peers will be sexually active, considering this as the norm.

2. Have some solid biblical, physical, and emotional reasons to wait for sex within marriage.

3. Know that being alone with a young person of the opposite sex can lead to unplanned intimacy, or even rape.

4. Know that there is a lot of room for creative interaction between being a lonely loner and going to bed with someone.

5. Work on expressing love without resorting to sexual intercourse by such other-centered actions as: giving flowers, being a good listener, having a caring attitude, which will build up the relationship far more than keeping it centered on the physical.

6. Plan creatively for dates. Go bowling, play ball, roller-skate, take walks, host parties, conduct a youth Bible study, take your pastor's kids to the zoo. All of these can be fun interaction and do keep both of you from long periods alone with nothing to do.

7. Beware of marrying anyone because they "need" you or because you are lonely.

8. Understand, accept, and be comfortable with their own sexuality.

One of the most urgent crises in the life of a young girl is that of suspecting she is pregnant, when her pregnancy is unwanted. Some young women are so distressed that they seriously consider suicide. It is important to check out the suspicion of pregnancy by using the simple pregnancy test that can be bought at most drugstores. Even if the test is positive, this could be a false reading and it should be rechecked by a good lab to confirm it. The young woman will need sensitive adults to help her deal with this crisis and choose the best option for handling an unwanted pregnancy.

If you think you are pregnant:
1. Most large drugstores sell inexpensive pregnancy test kits.
2. If you get a positive result, always have it rechecked by a lab, either at the college student health center or at a private physician's office.
3. School counselors or campus ministers will help you to deal with the crisis of an unwanted pregnancy. They are there to help you.
4. There are several options, and you can find the best one for you.
5. Do not despair.

Facing Discrimination

The racial tensions in the home countries are such a shock to "outsiders," not because discrimination does not exist elsewhere, but because a person in the culture becomes accustomed to its forms within that culture. MKs can often see their parents' home culture much more clearly than those who live in it. This is both good and bad: good in that she or he can help others recognize the discrimination she or he sees; bad in that a young MK does not often have the diplomacy to criticize in constructive ways. On the other hand, MKs who accept all people as equal, even "strange Americans, Britishers, Canadians or French," make a quiet and forceful statement against discrimination. As missionaries, we talk a lot about the world, but do we raise our children to be accepting and nonjudgmental of those who are different in appearance and in thought? MKs can become peacemakers between the various worlds that have become reconciled within themselves.

Suggestions:

1. Talk with your teenagers about discrimination.
2. Encourage them to see examples of people who are left out of the mainstream in your host country.
3. Discuss reasons why this exists.
4. Discuss the differences in discrimination and society's handling of dangerous elements (like drug pushers) for the safety of all.

Driving

A basic skill almost all young people in the developed nations have is driving. The law in many countries allows a sixteen-year-old to drive. Parents need to provide ways for their MKs to learn this skill before they leave home to be on their own. Whatever help is needed in order for the young person to get a driver's license is also a must. This does not mean that the MK needs to own a car. The skill and the license provide the possibility of driving, which some jobs require; identification required in many places; and a boost to the young person's feeling of worth in being on a par with her or his peers. If at all possible, make plans for your teenager to take a driver's education course. Some states require this for a young driver.

Knowing how to drive is important. Help your MK learn to drive, including how to drive on interstate highways and how to read maps. Look into the benefits of membership in AAA or other motor clubs.

Anyone 16 years of age or over should know how to drive. A driver's license is needed for:

(a) Driving. Some jobs require this skill.
(b) Identification. Often required to make a purchase or validate a check.
(c) Positive self-image. "Everyone has one." It's a sign of being an adult. It reminds the MK that she or he is able to function adequately in the new environment.

How to Wait

One useful but difficult how-to is how to wait—while one struggles through adjustment, frustration, and loneliness. It takes time to feel at home. A lot is happening at once: growing up, college, university, work, cross-cultural entry. Some tension is okay. This too shall pass, and in a year or two the MK will feel at home wherever she or he is.

1. Remember, an MK has some very strong pluses. (See pp. 83-84.)
2. Pick out one skill and put it to use in the new situation. MKs are observant. Join a bird-watcher group and enjoy the birds, and the people.
3. Keep in contact with former friends and other MKs who can encourage you.
4. Be available as a friend.
5. Realize others around you have much the same feelings as you.
6. Take part in a small support group in which you can find close friends. (See p. 121 for finding other MKs.) Your support group could be a small Bible study and prayer group, a small work group such as a committee in the dorm, or a sports team.
7. Spend time in Bible study and prayer, getting to know God better.
8. Look for the good around you in people and in circumstances.

Address, Please!

One of the questions MKs most dislike is, "Where are you from?" That is usually a conversation opener, so it can be expected when a new person arrives, but, for an unprepared MK, there is no easy answer.

"Am I from the last city I've been in, or from where my parents are now, or from where my last school was, or from where my grandparents live, or from the head office of my parents' mission, or where?"

The same confusion reigns when a form asks for "permanent address." "What is this 'permanent address' going to be used for? For mail, state residency, official document, credit or for something I can't even imagine?"

A helpful exercise during preparation for cross-cultural entry is to help an MK find possible answers to these questions. The answers may be changed as time goes along, as happened to an MK born in New Jersey and going to a New England college. When she was asked where she was from and answered, "New Jersey," her schoolmates would laugh and say, "What exit?" After several such put-downs, the MK decided the answer "Brazil" worked better in her situation.

Suggestions:

Where am I from?
1. Help your MK write down some possible answers to this question.
2. Gather addresses and phone numbers for the young person to keep for handy use.

MKs say to parents:

✔ *"Don't cut MKs off from what is happening in the U.S. Read U.S. news magazines, use videos to show U.S. dress, customs, etc."*

✔ *"Preparation for value differences is essential, for example, dancing."*

✔ *"Dress MKs like American kids."*

✔ *"Encourage research on biculturalism, especially the positive aspects."*

Work

One area of know-how that has plagued MKs is work. (See also work skills in Financial Management, Ch. 2.) In fact, one of the weaknesses of

MKs is that they do not know how to work. This does not mean that they are lazy. It means that on most mission fields there are few opportunities for teens to find employment such as their peers do during high school in the home country. Not only do the MKs not earn the money, but they also do not gain the independence and financial knowledge that go along with having a job. A job in the mission, often under the parents, does not usually teach the skills necessary for handling another culture independently.

One MK, in talking about people who influence changes in one's life, told of a family in the U.S. who sent him a plane ticket and gave him a job on their farm in the Midwest. He was part of their family that summer, made life-long friends, and learned the rewards of a hard day's work.

Investments

A young person, beginning to work, needs help in learning how to use and invest money. Seeing an investment multiply will be a very real learning experience. Your money can work for you. Even small amounts can be saved or invested. Ask your pastor or your financial aid officer for a referral to someone who can advise you on the handling of money.

While we are encouraging our MKs to go to our home country, get a job and earn money to help meet the study expenses, we are presenting them with a dilemma. "My parents don't work for money. Why should I?" This is a valid question to discuss with your MKs, pointing out that missionaries represent many workers who wish to share the gospel with the world.

Advice from MKs to MKs:
- ✔ *"Don't pig out on junk food." "Don't buy new clothes right away. You will probably gain weight and not be able to wear them." "Buy as many warm clothes as possible."*
- ✔ *"Act like an American—learn the 'language,' listen carefully, observe closely."*
- ✔ *"Keep abreast of current affairs in the U.S.; read in advance, especially secular magazines for youth; study recent American pop culture and history, see movies."*
- ✔ *"Learn how to put together a resume."*
- ✔ *"Come back to college early to work the summer."*

✔ *"Come to the U.S. for a summer during high school to work."*

✔ *"Study the culture, observe and absorb all that is around you—language, dress, styles, actions, etc.*

Notice that not all MKs agree. Some quotes contradict each other. Think about each point of view, and decide what is best in your situation.

Information That Helps

Teaching an MK how to do something is actually the easiest part of the job. A particular skill is decided upon, steps in performance are determined, and the skill is either practiced or theorized. The trick comes in determining ahead what sort of skills each MK will most need upon cross-cultural entry. Wise adults concentrate on skills that can be used in a variety of situations. An important part of the process is to learn to ask for help or explanations when needed. (Remember the lawn mower, p. 92?)

When a family enters together, as on a furlough, the parents could take the children along as they come across something new and ask for help in figuring it out. This could be finding the lint trap on a new dryer, or checking out the banks in order to open an account. MKs need to know it is okay not to know, even if most people around him or her seem to know all the answers. A long-term friend of the family would be a nonthreatening place to go for help.

Parents, remember to update about 25 years from when you went off to school and watch out for overload. Don't throw it all at the kids at once, or at the last minute!

Suggestions:

How to do something
1. Choose a skill.
2. Determine its steps.
3. Practice the skill, either in a real or mock situation.
4. Work on skills that can be used in a variety of situations.
5. Parents, remember to update your information.
6. Watch out for overload. A little planning can keep you from that last-minute cramming.

Information Source

1. Yellow Pages may have a "Christian Information" section. This lists jobs, care groups, etc.
2. "Shepherds Guide" is a listing of Christians in business and services. It can be found in Christian bookstores and churches.

"Am I in style?"

MKs Say

Give adequate family discussion time to those statements which seem applicable to your situation. Make sure everyone is heard. Take notes; make plans.

MKs say they need to know:

✔ *"How to use a telephone."*

✔ *"How to shop."*

✔ *"How to use a drinking fountain."*

✔ *"How to iron and other housekeeping duties."*

✔ *"How to use a bank."*

✔ *"How to dress and talk what is 'in,' slang."*

✔ *"American etiquette—how to say the right things when meeting new people; social customs."*

✔ *"Church habits, acceptance, culture; as well as understanding of other religions."*

✔ *"How to drive. How to call a taxi. The importance of a car. What to do on a freeway."*

✔ *"Dating customs, the dating system."*

✔ *"More about American geography, history, entertainers, etc."*

✔ *"That Americans are more event-oriented and less people-oriented; that they would seem to be provincial thinkers; about American racial discrimination."*

✔ *"That American people are wealthier than I ever imagined; the over-abundance in the U.S.; the emphasis on materialism."*

✔ *"That culture is different, not right or wrong."*

These are enough suggestions to keep adults and their MKs busy for many a moon. The essence seems to be not to lose touch with the culture in which MKs will be expected to function. There are many wonderful things about this world and there are also some very negative characteristics or trends. Young people need to be prepared to deal with both the good and the bad: not frightened, but prepared. Books and magazines, videos, more frequent trips, and parents interested in listening and learning with their young folk all contribute to better preparing the MK for cross-cultural entry.

Be prepared
Cross-cultural entry can be more fun for everyone. Learn about where you are going through books, magazines, videos, more frequent trips.

"Listen carefully, observe closely!"

Questions For Reflection

These questions can be used to help parents apply some of the material in the chapter to their own situation.

1. What are some safety rules you have taught in your home on the mission field?

2. How could this learning be transferred to situations encountered upon cross-cultural entry?

3. Why is knowing how to drive and having a driver's license so important to an 18-year-old MK returning to the parents' home country?

4. Make four statements describing present dating customs in your home country.

5. What could an MK do to get along well with someone who could be called a provincial thinker?

6. What are four ways in which your host country discriminates against minorities? Four ways in which your home country does the same?

7. Name five reasons a college freshman MK might pig out on junk food.

8. Name six kinds of people, other than MKs, who are bicultural.

9. What is your permanent address? Why did you choose it as your permanent address?

10. Why does a job in the parents' ministry usually not teach an MK what is learned by most young people working in your home country?

Work Sheets

What are some common denominators between people who have traveled internationally and those who haven't?

What are some major differences?

List five possible peer pressures. How can they best be handled?

1.

2.

3.

4.

5.

What is the purpose of money? In what ways can it be helpful? When is it harmful?

Exercise 1: BE A DETECTIVE

Imagine you are an 18-year-old returning to your parents' home country for college or work. What clues will you have to help you in the new situation? (This exercise can be adapted for any age MK.)

WHO are you?
Give some of the characteristics you see in yourself that reflect your host country and some which reflect your parents' home country.

WHERE are you from?
List your possible addresses. In what situations would each one be useful?

WHAT do you need?

A. What job could you try to get that would help you prepare for living on your own?

B. What are four situations in which you would use a driver's license?

C. What are five of your favorite foods? What would you consider five "junk" foods? What are three reasons a young person might overindulge in "junk" foods?

D. WHEN is it important to ask for help?

E. HOW do you go about asking for help?

5

Relationships

We mortals need one another
in order to be fully human.
—S.D. Goede

I grew up on the mission field among dozens of mission "aunts" and "uncles." True, they were all spread over the country's vast expanse and usually saw each other only once a year at the mission retreat. There was, however, a real sense of kinship, love and responsibility for each other.

In my teens, I began to leave off childish ways. As a part of what I considered "being adult," I decided that using "aunt" and "uncle" for people who were not my blood relatives was kids' stuff, and not for me any more.

A little while later I was visiting in another missionary home and cheerfully greeted the hosts with, "Hello, Dr. Smith. Hello, Mrs. Smith. I'm so glad to see you again."

"Why, Alma!" Mrs. Smith responded. "Don't you even know who your real aunt and uncle are?"

For the above MK, there were many mission aunts and uncles, among whom there were also blood relatives. During her growing-up years no difference had been made among them, for all were part of a large family. As she began to see herself as a separate person and began to look for ways in which to relate to others, she found it was not always easy to get close to people, and that she had much to learn about the effective building of relationships.

How to deal with people is a major issue for cross-cultural entry MKs of any age, but especially for late teens beginning a separate life from their families. At this point in their lives they are moving from a tight-knit group to a sea of loose acquaintances. This fact alone requires a new set of guidelines for relationships.

Communication

When to talk and what to say is a difficult art for anyone to learn. For an entering young person, this can be especially confusing. Some of the more outgoing personalities cover up for their uncertainty by talking nonstop. They talk so much, and about subjects for which their peers have no frame of reference, that soon they find themselves talking alone. The shy MKs wait around to be asked about their experiences, and they too can end up alone, an enigma to their peers.

A young person who feels comfortable with self has a valuable beginning toward sound relationships with others. Once an MK is sure that people from New Jersey, Brazil, or Boston are created equal, that MK is free to stop defending ground and begin making friends.

What an MK says can so often be misunderstood. Here are two examples: "The MAID at home . . ." or, "When I was in PARIS last summer . . ."

"A home away from home helps."

Wise MKs use caution in speech so that others won't think they are showing off. "The MAID at home . . ." and "When I was in PARIS . . ." are statements that don't make friends.

Many Americans, based on life in the United States, would interpret such statements as showing off, or having a wealthy life-style, when in reality having help at home is usual in many countries and is often as much an asset to the worker as it is to the family. Being in Paris does sound exotic, but how can you not be there if that is where you live? It is wise, however, for MKs to use some caution in the way they say things, at least until they become a real part of a group of peers. They do not need immediately to tell everyone else what they think or what they believe.

Getting along well with others also invariably requires unselfishness. The individual's goal needs to be somewhere outside self. This characteristic is learned in little segments from infancy on, often through hard experience. If a child does not want to share the ball, there may be no children left with whom to play.

In helping children build healthy relationships, parents can teach them to think through a crisis rather that just reacting emotionally. In a play-acting situation, children could pretend that a friend took away their ball. The children then think about what it feels like to get mad. They get hot and tense, and their breathing speeds up. They are then taught to slow down their breathing and think words such as, "I am mad," "Jim took my ball," "I want Jim to play with me," "I guess I'll share the ball."

This practice can help the children to deal with the next real conflict in ways that are constructive to the relationship. Small children often cannot easily put their thoughts and feelings into words. If the child looks like she or he wants something, but does not ask, help him or her to verbalize the thought. For example, "You look like you want something. If you want something, just come and ask." In these ways children can be helped to communicate better.

If parents write down some of the things their children say when they are small, these notes can help the young person understand his or her feelings later. Art work can serve the same purpose. Keeping the MK's letters from boarding school gives parents an advantage on keeping memories.

Parents have a tendency toward wanting to protect their children, and sometimes they cut off some learning experiences. The high school gang comes over for games and snacks and leaves the kitchen in a mess. Quite late, when the last friend is gone, mother hugs her child and says, "You go on to bed, dear. You have to be up early and you need your sleep. I'll clean up."

There might be an occasional instance in which that is a help. Usually it teaches the young person that actions do not have consequences and that the world revolves around "me." This can be a real handicap in relationships upon cross-cultural entry and can hinder learning to live alone effectively as a young adult.

Parents, Let Your Kids Grow up!

Henry Brandt has some wise words for parents: "Parents drive themselves crazy trying to make their children happy. You cannot give your children joy. Only God can."

In preparing young people for relationships on an adult level, we need to help them have the good sense to bide their time; listen more than talk; share present feelings rather than experiences they had overseas.

Relationship With Parents

Relationships with parents are bound to change when the MK leaves for college. The great distances usually involved, and the different worlds in which the family members will then live, add to the complexity of the situation. Even though today's technology does much to help keep people in touch, there is a gap to be bridged that takes working at by both young people and parents. One MK wrote:

"You can't write letters to your parents when you are down because it takes so long for mail to get home and for your folks to answer that the problem is all over by then."

Often MKs are primed to be people-pleasers, and they don't want to upset parents or people around them. Somehow they need to find people with whom they can share honest feelings, both positive and negative. They need to be reassured that they are accepted and loved the way they are. Many times faraway parents are helpful to other peoples' children and need to trust that someone will be there for their own MKs. Is this so different from people in other walks of life?

Adult MKs (AMKs) often carry in themselves hurts they have never felt free to talk about with their parents. They need to find ways to openly share the pain of feeling abandoned, or of rebelling against the many moves, or of whatever they have held against their parents since childhood. Forgiveness on both sides brings healing and a new closeness to the relationship. Parents can help this happen by being willing to talk about difficult issues.

Dealing with anger, disagreement and frustration is not a skill easily learned on the mission field where everyone is supposed to be nice to everyone else. For an MK to leave home not having learned how to fight constructively is a handicap. Following are some basic guidelines that your family could work on when involved in an argument.

BOTH SIDES CAN WIN AN ARGUMENT

1. Stick to a single issue and avoid past grievances.
2. Do not attack in words or actions.
3. Be honest.
4. Listen.
5. Do not fight in public.
6. Don't threaten to end the relationship.
7. Don't walk out in the middle of an argument.
8. Apologize when wrong.
9. Compromise.
10. Don't hold a grudge.

Loving is much more than just being sweet. It is also being willing to admit there is a difference of opinion and being willing to talk it out. Even though the confrontation is scary, it is healing if done by the rules above. It also frees the participants to continue a creative and maturing relationship.

An MK is strengthened by this kind of relationship with his or her parents, and with others along the way who become significant in her or his life.

Everyone needs people who are friends, on the same level, not authorities. An MK said, "I hold people off by my actions and words, and if people are willing to go over my barrier, then I believe they are interested in me, and I trust them."

Cross-cultural entry is often so unsettling that an MK might easily resort to the above action. It is not the quickest road to making friends; there need to be people around who can relate to such a person whose world is upside down. Encourage your MK to actively seek out upperclass MKs and ask for help.

The most reiterated statement from MKs is, "MKs can best help other MKs." There is no one like another one to understand one.

School administrators, church leaders, and other monocultural adults in the home countries often group MKs and international students together. There are some obvious characteristics in common—experience in other countries, acceptance of people who are different, a variety of languages. The MK can be a bridge between the foreign students and the new culture to which these students are adapting.

However, it is important to take into account a major difference. The international students look like they come from another culture, act like they come from another culture, and are accepted in the new environment as international guests.

MKs look like those around them, and even though they act rather strangely, they are expected to know what young people in that culture take for granted. MKs are not international students, but a blend of local and foreign culture. They can be friends to international students, but at the same time they need a support group that understands their multicultural characteristics.

Encourage MKs to get together. Provide some extra money for letters, phone calls and occasional trips.

Helping MKs stay in contact with other MKs is well worth the trouble or expense. It is important to encourage them to do so. When an MK's mother died, the parents of another MK sent their daughter a check for weekly phone calls across the country so that the two friends could share this very difficult experience. MKs have a running start in relating to one another. They speak the same "language" even when coming from all corners of the earth.

Letters

Letters cannot be overstressed as a lifeline to and from an entering MK. That some parents need to be reminded to write their kids seems sad. Any missionary should be able to remember those first few months on the mission field when letters from home filled such a big void in their hearts. The young adult MK is feeling much the same dislocation, and news from family and friends soothes her or his longing.

Start practicing. Like prayer, writing letters is an important investment in your MK.

Young people also find writing letters to be a way of expressing their feelings and of maintaining ties with family and old friends. Some need to be reminded that parents need letters just as much as children do. Life tends to get busy, and the MK sometimes plans to write parents "tomorrow," but "tomorrow" comes less and less frequently. It helps to remember that writing letters can become a habit that, once established, does not take a great deal of effort, just some thoughtfulness. Letters do not have to be words on paper. They can be spoken through cassette tapes. It is great fun to hear a voice across the miles. Ironically, too many letters written during those first cross-cultural entry months by homesick MKs will take time that they should be using to make new friends. Keeping a balanced perspective even in this will help an MK adjust well.

LETTERS CAN:

- Encourage.
- Tickle your "funny bone."
- Support.
- Console.
- Bring on temporary homesickness.
- Banish homesickness.
- Bring joy.
- Communicate.
- Bring you closer.
- Give news.
- Make the receiver feel loved.
- Strengthen family ties.
- Are a ministry. (See also "Keeping in Touch, Ch. 1.)

LETTERS CAN BE:

- Pen on paper.
- Voice on cassette tape.
- Video.
- Fax.
- Night-letter telegram.

The following "MKs SAY" can provide a starting place for young people beginning to relate to others on an adult level.

MKs Say

Give adequate family discussion time to those statements which seem applicable to your situation. Make sure everyone is heard. Take notes; make plans.

MKs say they would like to have known:

✔ *"Of the need for me to initiate friendships."*

✔ *"That my parents weren't 100% right or 100% wrong."*

✔ *"That you need to get along with others even if you do not want to live like them."*

MKs say to MKs:

✔ *"Seek out other MKs for support; keep up MK relationships (telephone or write;) attending a college where there are other MKs is helpful."*

✔ *"Know your relatives in the U.S. ahead of time."*

✔ *"Have at least one key person with whom a solid relationship has been established ahead of time. Have someone you can be accountable to."*

✔ *"Take time to make friends; let nearby missionary families help you; be interested in others and try to meet people."*

✔ *"Find a friend you can trust (and ask stupid questions of). Don't be afraid to ask questions. Adopt someone who can be a stabilizing influence. If you have personal problems, talk to someone you can trust."*

✔ *"Get involved in a small group—find good people you can confide in (a support group)—find a good church."*

✔ *"Don't expect people to be interested in your 'jungle' stories; talk about yourself and your background only when it is appropriate."*

✔ *"Don't expect friendships to be the same as Brazilian friendships."*

MKs say to parents and missions:

✔ *"Keep the family in touch with what is happening in the U.S."*

✔ *"Locate missionaries in the U.S. who will extend themselves to MKs reentering; maintain mission ties on the field, as colleagues serve as extended family for the MKs."*

✔ *"Encourage a network of 'homes' away from home by passing on names and phone numbers of family friends near the college or work."*

✔ *"Getting MKs together is therapeutic—encourage your kids to keep in touch with other MKs."*

✔ *"Periodic retreats for MKs (over holidays) would be helpful. Have present a trained counselor who knows MKs. Include lots of free time and MK interaction. Send out a list of participants in advance so kids can look forward to being together."*

Setting up a Support Group

How to go about setting up a support group in a college.

1. Look for other MKs.
   Check with the registrar for students from other countries.
   Check students in the language courses.
   Check area churches for students from overseas.
   Check with the international students organization
2. Look for a professor or staff member who might be interested in being a sponsor for your group.
3. Write to Mu Kappa (see address in Appendix A) for literature and ideas.
4. Find a local church interested in helping your group with such things as finding homes for the holidays, helping with shopping, and community services.
5. Get together periodically for listening to each other and for fun activities, such as preparing and sharing a meal typical of a host country.
6. Help incoming MKs in adjusting to college life and to living in a new country.

How an adult can set up a support group
in a city, or work situation.

1. Advertise in the local newspaper the place and date for a meeting open to all MKs. For safety, the location for this first meeting should probably be a public place such as a school auditorium or a library.
2. Look for large churches in the nearest metropolitan area and ask them to put an ad for an MK gathering in their newsletter or on a bulletin board.
3. Find a local group like Rotary Club or a community college whose members would be willing to sponsor and host a periodic gathering of MKs.
4. Invite special speakers like psychologists, experts in overseas countries/areas, investment specialists, political scientists, educators, church leaders, writers, or diplomatic corps members.
5. Use the meetings for fellowship, learning and helping each other handle cross-cultural transition issues.

Relationships are a big factor in the adjustment of entering MKs. As a whole, MKs have learned many skills with which to deal with people. Cross-cultural entry in their late teens will reinforce some of these skills and eliminate others, helping the majority of MKs become a unique asset in being able to deal with people of all nations.

Questions For Reflection

These questions can be used to help parents apply some of the material in the chapter to their own situation.

1. Name ten away-from-home MKs from your mission. Where are they? Give a personal detail about each one (such as "Doris enjoys playing the piano.")

2. Outline a plan for your MK to know and be known by a member of your family who would be likely to care about the MK, and be of help during his or her college years.

3. How can a parent help a cross-cultural entry MK find a church home?

4. How are friendships in your home country different from those in your host country for your MK?

5. How can parents and their away-from-home MKs share problems, given the time lag in the mail?

6. List four significant people in your life and add one reason as to why each one was/is important.

7. Give five "do's" to include in letters to your MK. List five "don'ts."

Work Sheets

How can a parent help a cross-cultural MK find a church home upon re-entry to the parents' home country?

_____

_____

How can parents and their away-from-home MKs share problems, given the time lag in the mail?

_____

_____

_____

How are friendships different in the host country and the home country?

_____

_____

_____

How can you cultivate a special friendship between an MK and an extended family member (cousin, aunt, uncle, etc.) in preparation for the college years?

_____

_____

_____

Exercise 1: FACTS AND FIGURES

Instructions: Fill in the following, then compare with the others in your group.

A. Name three MKs you know, where they are, and one fact about each one.

B. List four people who have greatly influenced you. Why?

6

Tools That Have Helped Upon Cross-Cultural Entry

> If you may have in your life one or two
> real friends you are very wealthy.
> —S.D. Gordon

When I first went to college, I was dropped off at school late one afternoon as a cold wind blew across the campus. Just before the staff went home for the night, I was assigned to a dorm. A worker let me in the bare room, and, reminding me that the cafeteria would open only the next day, hurriedly left the building, her steps echoing down the hall.

I looked around for my footlocker that had been sent ahead. No sign of it. That meant nothing with which to make up the bed. I looked out the window at a gray, deserted campus. Town, I remembered, was ten miles away. Through the broken windowpane, rain was beginning to splatter in.

Tired, cold, hungry and utterly alone, I stretched out on the scrubby mattress and fell asleep.

This MK did not have many tools to help her on her first night at college.

Counseling

Of the several hundred MKs polled, all but three mentioned a list of things, people, and situations that helped them in adjusting to their parents' culture. Those who felt they had no help said, "No one helped me. I had to endure, observe, and learn fast." "I had no tools and I crashed."

Undoubtedly others, who did not get enough help on cross-cultural entry, did not respond to the questionnaire. A few have been desperate enough to kill themselves.

Others, who have faced major and minor crises, strongly recommend professional counseling. One MK goes so far as to say all MKs would benefit from talking with a professional counselor sometime in their college years. It has helped her sort out questions she didn't know were bothering her. Almost all schools have a school counselor. Many colleges and universities have low-cost or free counseling.

There are many Christian professional counselors today from whom to choose. It is important that the counselor know something about MKs and their blend of cultures. It is helpful to realize that if talking to one counselor for a few sessions does not help, a young person is perfectly free to look for another. Each person is responsible for himself or herself and needs to go after what is crucial not only to survival, but also to wholeness.

CHRISTIAN PROFESSIONAL COUNSELING

—Is not only for "crazy" people.
—Is not a black mark on someone's reputation.
—Is not only for those who are very sick.
—Is a help for anyone in thinking through what they feel.
—Is a help in sorting out questions.
—Is a help to MKs, all of whom need to come to terms with their
  multicultural backgrounds.

Often, family counseling is the key to helping an MK find answers to crucial questions. Parents and mission administrators need to be alert to this possible need and be willing to work out the logistics of bringing it about.

There are several cross-cultural transition seminars (reentry seminars) being offered in North America for high school and college students who are entering the parents' home culture for school or work. At these seminars, caring, experienced, and competent personnel provide information, testing, personal counsel, and an array of practical experiences in North American daily life. Beyond the structured benefits of such a gathering, many MKs say their favorite aspect of the seminar is the coming together of MKs from all over the world for a very special time of sharing. Attending one of these seminars should be seriously considered by all families who are sending their teen children to live in the parents' home country.

(See resources at the end of this book for addresses of cross-cultural entry programs, also known as reentry seminars.)

People were remembered as the single biggest help to MKs upon cross-cultural entry.

Caring teachers make a difference.

MKs found helpful:

- ✔ "Other MKs."
- ✔ "Friends."
- ✔ "Relatives."
- ✔ "Brother/sister."
- ✔ "Living with my brother."
- ✔ "Parents."
- ✔ "Family keeping in touch."
- ✔ "Former missionaries in the U.S."
- ✔ "Friends of parents."
- ✔ "College mentors (staff, professors, friends)."
- ✔ "Brazilians in the U.S."
- ✔ "Brazilian friends."
- ✔ "Letters."
- ✔ "Athletics—team activity."
- ✔ "Local supporting church that helped with finances, transportation and just being there."
- ✔ "Youth groups."
- ✔ "Church peer groups."
- ✔ "Other Christians."
- ✔ "Interest groups at school"
- ✔ "Interaction between school and church."

"Are we having fun yet?"

Preparation in Crucial Areas

Young people who leave their parents' home on the mission field to go back to living in the midst of their parents' home culture face a drastic change. One MK said, "Have you talked to your kids about sex and drugs and alcohol and AIDS? You have to, you know. Don't be embarrassed. They need to know the facts." In today's world parents need facts in all these areas and many more, even if they do live in Irian Jaya!

Tobacco

The smoking of tobacco products is the chief avoidable cause of death in our society. Some 30 percent of cancer deaths are linked to smoking.[1] Smokeless tobacco (chewing, snuff, etc.) is equally harmful. Today tobacco and alcohol are known to be "starter drugs," leading to the use of even more dangerous drugs such as cocaine.

In North America public perception has changed in recent years, so that smoking is now considered harmful to the smoker and the environment. Increasingly, public places such as government buildings, hospitals, many work places, public conveyances, etc., are designated "nonsmoking" areas.

Disadvantages of Smoking

1. Contributes to lung and heart diseases, including cancer.
2. Produces smokers' cough.
3. Decreases sense of taste.
4. Causes offensive odor.
5. Discolors teeth.
6. Pollutes surrounding air ("second-hand smoke").
7. During pregnancy contributes to lower birth weight and respiratory problems in the baby.
8. Is an expensive habit.
9. Proven addictive. Very hard to stop.

Alcohol

Alcohol abuse remains America's number one drug problem. Alcohol for drinking is readily available and is legal in many states for those 21 years of age or over; in some states the legal age is 18. Alcohol is so common that many people don't realize it's a powerful drug. They drink before they think. Heavy drinking over a period of years damages both body (cirrhosis of the liver, stomach ulcers) and mind (black outs, losing touch with reality).

Mixing alcohol and drugs with driving has contributed dramatically to the number one youth killer—accidents—and the statistics are escalating. Even small amounts of alcohol significantly impair the judgment and coordination required to drive a car safely. You will not be in control of your actions when intoxicated. When you are driving, if you are stopped by the police and tested for the presence of alcohol in your blood, there will be heavy penalties for even 0.1% alcohol.

Remember, you can get help for yourself and/or your friends through a school counselor or Alcoholics Anonymous (AA.) Look in the white pages of the phone book under "alcohol" or "alcoholism."

For more information and referrals for problems of alcoholism or drugs, call toll free 1-800- NCA-CALL (National Council on Alcoholism Information Line.)

If you choose not to drink:
1. Trust your reasons. Don't get talked into "just this once."
2. Don't apologize. Just say "No thanks."
3. Plan your activities so that alcohol won't be a major part of the entertainment.
4. Respect others who drink. Don't sneer or act superior.

Drugs

Two of the most effective prevention tools parents have against substance abuse of any kind are awareness of the problem and knowledge of ways to help motivate their children to resist the pressure to use alcohol and other drugs.

Illegal use of drugs such as cannabis (marijuana), inhalants (like laughing gas), cocaine (or crack), stimulants (like speed), depressants (downers), hallucinogens (like PCP and LSD), narcotics (like heroin), designer drugs (illegal drugs modified by underground chemists), anabolic steroids (sometimes used in sports programs) is dangerous to health, habit forming, and can land the user in jail.[2]

Slang names for drugs change frequently. Your school will probably have drug education pamphlets that will help you.

For more information write:
The National Clearinghouse for Alcohol and Drug Information, P.O. Box 2345, Rockville, MD, 20852. Telephone (301) 468-2600.

24-Hour Hot Line: National Institute on Drug Abuse
(Toll free) 1-800-662-HELP.

AIDS

AIDS stands for acquired immunodeficiency syndrome, a breakdown of the body's immune system. This system fights off infections and certain other diseases, therefore its breakdown leaves the body wide open to life-threatening illness. HIV is the human immunodeficiency virus which causes AIDS and can be detected by blood test. An apparently healthy person can have the HIV in their body for a year or two, or even ten years before symptoms appear. In 1989 more than 18,000 people aged 20 to 29 had been diagnosed with AIDS.[3]

There are two main ways that people become infected with HIV:
1. By engaging in sexual intercourse with an infected person.
2. By sharing drug needles or syringes with an infected person.

Mistreating the body through use of drugs (legal or illegal) and promiscuous sex are dangerous predisposing factors. The ingestion of harmful foods and living in overly stressful situations can also lower the body's resistance to infection.

HIV is NOT spread by coughs and sneezes, telephones, clothes, or toilet seats. AIDS is NOT transmitted through normal everyday contact.

How to avoid AIDS
1. Don't have sex with an infected person. Remember, often you can't tell whether a person is infected or not.
2. If in doubt, don't have sex.
3. Don't do drugs.

The use of latex condoms has been widely recommended as a means of "safe sex," but they must be used properly every time, and be made of latex rubber which serves as a barrier to the virus. Condoms are a preventive measure against AIDS, but are far from foolproof.

Free AIDS pretest counseling and testing are available at almost all public health departments. Tentative results can be available in 24 hours and more definitive results in three weeks.

Alert: Sometimes results are false positive.

Another option:
National AIDS Hotline. Call toll free 1-800-342-AIDS for information and an address where you can go in your area to get counseling about an HIV test.

Upon cross-cultural entry MKs will be faced with decisions in many crucial areas, including the use of tobacco, alcohol, drugs, and sexual contacts that could lead to AIDS. Knowing something about these subjects will help young people to make wise choices.

As in all of life, however, there will be times when poor choices are made. If kids get in trouble, do you ask them Why? and then listen, really listen, to their answers? Do you refuse to be part of the mission field gossip hotline and not pass on such tidbits as, "Did you know Freddy is drinking?" or "Have you heard about Polly?" or "Isn't it too bad about Joe!"

That kind of talk hurts and certainly does not help anyone. It is deadly for MKs. They are not around to defend themselves. MKs need your support, like writing them a letter, encouraging them, and, if need be, forgiving them. MKs need to see that the adults around them are pilgrims, too, that they are authentic people who need forgiveness and love. To this, MKs can relate.

Have you written an MK today?

Suggestion:

The mission family helps MKs by writing letters to them, encouraging them, and sharing with them as authentic people.

MKs Say

Give adequate family discussion time to those statements which seem applicable to your situation. Make sure everyone is heard. Take notes, make plans.

MKs say this is helpful:

- ✔ *"Parents' understanding when I had problems."*
- ✔ *"Teachers who valued me."*
- ✔ *"Opportunities for sharing my experiences that helped me keep them as an ongoing thing and not something that was over."*
- ✔ *"MK retreat."*
- ✔ *"Cross-cultural entry program."*
- ✔ *"Cross-cultural communications course."*
- ✔ *"An article by an MK in a Wycliffe publication."*

"We speak the same memories."

✔ *"Help with landing a summer job."*

✔ *"Missionary boutique (used clothes) that supplied nice clothes."*

✔ *"The Bible and prayer."*

✔ *"'Spiritual parents" in the U.S."*

✔ *"Good educational habits."*

✔ *"Knowing English well."*

✔ *"Mission publications with helpful articles."*

✔ *"Books," "American magazines," "TV," "Christian literature," "cross-cultural literature."*

✔ *"A positive attitude."*

Advantages of a Missionary Family

Families rearing children today have serious problems with which to contend. Children are bombarded with values, some of which could seriously be questioned. In many places the home, an important place of stability and permanence for children, has begun to crumble. While these things are happening in society at large, missionary families in most cases have several often unnoticed advantages.

The first and most important is a strong faith in God, strong enough to have brought the family out of its natural environment and into a culture distant not only in miles, but also in its customs. This faith is a great help in holding the family together and in making the family members into a team. The children are provided with an unusually stable environment within the home and with a sense of being worthwhile as they contribute to the family's ministry.

The second is that most missionary families live apart from Western industrialized society. The early childhood years can be spent learning some lessons about life, such as how to create your own fun, how to live close to nature as when fishing for dinner, and how to make choices on the use of time since often there are few programmed activities (clubs, organized sports, and TV) for the family members.

The simple life style on many mission fields can teach children:
   How to create their own fun.
   How to live close to nature.
   How to make wise choices.

MKs say family preparation and planning provided some of the tools for MKs

✔ *"Special family times together during parents' furlough."*

✔ *"Parents' furlough during high school years."*

✔ *"Parents' furlough the year I reentered."*

✔ *"The preparation my parents gave me."*

✔ *"Having time in the parents' home country before starting college."*

Music

Growing up surrounded by music in many forms is one of the special pluses of missionary families. The missionary work force has a larger than average percentage of members with musical ability. Christian leadership involves singing and instrumental music and the church is a training ground for "making a joyful sound." The heritage of generations of beautiful church music belongs to all Christians.

When spoken language is a barrier, music reaches across to communicate in a language of love and fellowship. In the absence of high-tech professional equipment, common people with a little talent spend time and effort to learn to play an instrument for the pleasure it provides to the musician and to those around him or her.

When your MK leaves home, music can comfort, help to make friends, and be the door to groups such as chorale, band, singing groups, and orchestra.

MAKING MUSIC IN YOUR FAMILY

—Sing often.

—Encourage each child to learn to play one or more instruments.

—Play classical music in the home.

—As your children become teens, listen to the music of their generation with them.

—Help your children to know how to evaluate different types of music.

—Enjoy music together.

When it's Time to go

Eventually the children will need to leave home to seek their own place in the world. The transition will have its aches and pitfalls, but there is a good chance that the MK will enter the adult world with an inner self that is equipped to withstand the storms of life.

An MK was asked to name what was most important to an MK. Here is the answer: "Lots of love and attention. Freedom to make choices such as education, where to live, etc. Encouragement to read, and plenty of English books."

The "MKs SAY" sections in this book are valuable starting points in encouraging MKs to become creative, mature adults. Remember, MKs have usually acquired a second language naturally. Their seasoned maturity is generally a product of different environments and the leadership style of their parents. They are often excellent observers, noticing detail that escapes others. They know there is much to learn, having experienced a variety of living styles. These trans-cultural kids are trained to adapt to new places and are valuable in multinational situations. In fact, rather than perceiving the world as flat, they see it in its real dimensions and living color. MKs are people who are often very caring of others, and who have seen God in action in many critical situations.

This book dwells on the hard spots in hopes of making them better learning situations. But there is a whole wonderful world of experiences open to MKs, and most of us would not trade our MKness for anything else.

End Notes

1. *Growing Up Drug Free.* (Washington, D.C.: U.S. Department of Education, 1989.)

2. *Growing Up Drug Free,* op. cit.

3. *AIDS Prevention Guide,* Box 6003, Rockville, Md. 20850. Telephone 1-800-324-AIDS.

Missionary Kid Beatitudes
(By a sophomore MK in Ivory Coast, West Africa)

Blessed is the MK who understands that where he is and what he has is God's will, for he will be content.

Blessed is the MK who makes friends quickly, for he will enjoy furlough more.

Blessed is the MK who enjoys traveling, because traveling is a constant part of his life.

Blessed is the MK who enjoys being with his parents and siblings, for they are sometimes the only friends he has.

Blessed is the MK who learns a lot about the language and culture where he grows up, for it can help him in later life.

Blessed is the MK who keeps up with what's happening in the States or Canada, for he won't be culture-shocked when he returns.

Blessed is the MK who takes advantage of where he is, for he has a lot of unique opportunities and experiences.

Blessed is the MK who has "rich" relatives in the States, for they may send him clothes, music, books, etc.

Blessed is the MK who realizes how lucky and special he is and how God chose him or her specifically for this role in life, for he shall be blessed later in life by the fact that he grew up an MK.

Questions For Reflection

These questions can be used to help parents apply some of the material in the chapter to their own situation.

1. What are some ways in which you could help churches in your home country relate to your MKs?

2. Suggest three possible "special family times" for a furlough.

3. List five ways that a teacher can show that she or he values the student.

4. Give three examples of situations in which you think an MK would feel comfortable sharing his or her experiences.

5. Suggest some ways in which English books (or books in your native tongue) could get into the hands of isolated MKs.

6. What is the most significant factor in forming a positive attitude in a person?

7. What would be an answer to, "Did you know Freddy is drinking?"

8. Name some tools that have helped your MK in cross-cultural entry.

Work Sheets

When should an MK seek counseling?

How does the fear of AIDS change interpersonal relationships?

Are some kinds of music detrimental? Explain. What makes music beneficial?

Exercise 1: THE RACE

Instructions: This game is best played by two or more groups. To begin, place markers at START and advance as each question is answered. The objective is to discuss cross-cultural entry situations. To score, give one point for each answer. Add two bonus points for completion of each number. No points for bypassing stops. There is a possible total of 40 points.

Total points:	**35 to 40:**	**You understand MKs.**
	25 to 35:	**Cross-cultural entry visa on hold.**
	below 25:	**Go read the book again.**

1. What are three ways you could help your churches back home relate to MKs? Advance one square for each way. As a bonus advance two more spaces. If no examples come to mind, go directly to the church to think about it, then advance two spaces.

2. Suggest two possible "special family times" for a furlough. Advance two spaces.

3. List five ways a teacher can show that she or he values the student. Advance one space on detour.

4. Advance one space for each of three examples of situations where MKs would feel comfortable sharing their experiences.

5. Suggest ways English books can get to isolated MKs. Advance one space for each suggestion, up to three.

6. Gossip in the air! Advance one space if you can suggest two ways to stop it. If not, return to DEEP PIT and reread Chapter VI while the others continue.

7. If you can name a significant factor in forming a positive attitude in a person, advance to the prize. If not, return to the church and think about it. Try the race again another day.

8. Name five tools that have helped MKs reenter. Go to the FINISH and total your points.

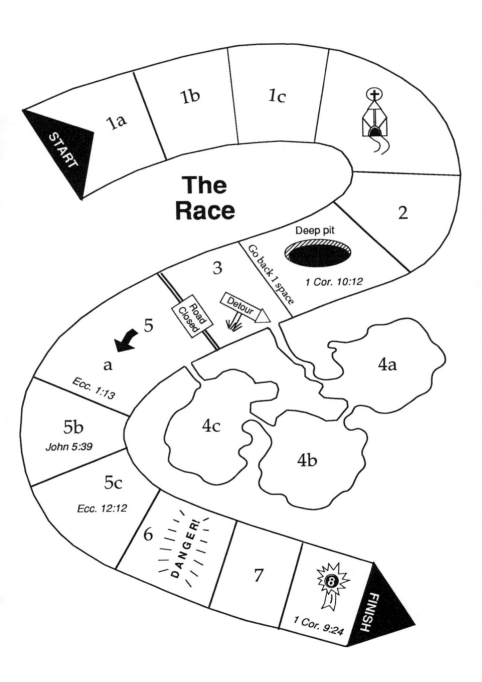

Appendices

Appendix A

Mu Kappa International

Mu Kappa International is a unique new ministry organized by MKs themselves specifically to address their own felt needs. "By MKs for MKs" aptly describes its overriding focus.

Mu Kappa (Greek letters for M and K) began in 1986 on the campus of Taylor University in Upland, Indiana. Member chapters are now expanding to many other college campuses across the U.S.

The purpose of Mu Kappa International is to help MKs in their cultural transitions; to promote growth, unity and Christian fellowship among chapter members; and to help coordinate the efforts of missions and paramission organizations to maximize the potential of the over 30,000 MKs.

Mu Kappa International helped sponsor the historic "MK Gathering" at Urbana '87 with nearly four hundred MKs in attendance. The Mu Kappa concept was received with enthusiasm.

Mu Kappa International has many potential aspects of ministry:
1. College campus chapters.
2. Adult chapters (post-college).
3. Big brother-big sister concept.
4. International publications.
5. High adventure programs.
6. Conferences—regional, national, international.
7. Networking services geared to the needs of MKs.
   a. Career planning.
   b. "Cities of Refuge" for troubled MKs.
   c. Cross-cultural transition programs.
   d. Financial information.
   e. Pre-field training of MKs going abroad.
   f. Missions outreach opportunities.
   g. Travel information.
   h. Local church involvement.

For more information contact Mu Kappa International, Box 1388, Desoto, Tex. 75115. Jim Lauer, director. Telephone (214) 230-1710.

Appendix B

(Appendices B through J are adapted from material presented by Interfaces (International Family and Children's Educational Services) at the Overseas Ministries Study Center, New Haven, Conn., November, 1988.)

Questions for cross-cultural entry

Joan Wilson of the Foreign Service Institute of the U.S. Department of State has compiled a list of questions to ask when learning about another country. The following list is an adaptation that can be used by missionary families who are preparing to return home:

1. How many people, who are prominent in the affairs of your home country or state, can you name (political, athletics, religion, the arts, etc.)?

2. Who are some of the national heroes and heroines of your home country?

3. Do you know the national anthem? Pledge of Allegiance?

4. What is the predominant denomination or religion in the area where you'll be? What do you know about it?

5. How do members of the predominant denomination or religion feel about others?

6. How are marriages performed and celebrated?

7. What are attitudes toward divorce?

8. What is the attitude toward gambling?

9. What is the attitude toward drinking? Drugs?

10. Can you ever bargain over the prices of merchandise? If yes, where can this be done?

11. Can you pick up and handle merchandise?

12. What is the normal meal schedule?

13. What is the custom for visiting friends?

14. What foods are popular?

15. What is the usual dress for school? Do teenagers wear jeans?

16. Do you have to make appointments for haircuts?

17. What are the special privileges of age or sex?

18. If you are invited to dinner, when should you arrive?

19. On what occasions would you be expected to take gifts?
20. How do people greet one another?
21. How do people take leave of one another?
22. What are the important holidays and how are they observed?
23. What are the favorite leisure and recreational activities?
24. What sports are popular?
25. What TV shows are popular? Why?
26. What games do children play?
27. Where do young people congregate?
28. How are children disciplined?
29. Are children present at social occasions? What about baby-sitters?
30. What kind of public transportation is available?
31. Who has the right-of-way in traffic?
32. What are the large circulation newspapers in the area?
33. What kind of health services are available? Where are these located?
34. What are common home remedies?
35. Where are medicines purchased?
36. What are the public schools like?
37. How do these schools compare to others?
38. What schools are considered best?
39. Are children restricted to specific schools by the family's address?
40. Are there colleges and universities in the area?
41. Are there museums in the area?
42. What are the opportunities for arts and music involvement and/or appreciation?
43. What are the tourist attractions in the area?
44. Do teenagers work? What job possibilities are available to teenagers?
45. How late and how early in the day is it customary to phone someone?

In other words, treat your return to the home country much the same way as you prepared (or would prepare) for going to your first overseas assignment.

Appendix C

Ways *parents* can help MKs in cross-cultural entry

1. Monitor your own attitude; communicate a positive, happy outlook.
2. Be sensitive and responsive to children's stresses and needs.
3. In a sensitive way, share your own struggles in cultural adjustments with the children.
4. Talk the children through the "culture-shock" cycle: honeymoon, disillusionment, endurance, enjoyment. Help them to identify and talk about their love-hate feelings. Be sensitive but honest.
5. Demonstrate your love and concern for them.
6. Every culture has good and bad aspects. From a biblical point of view, discuss with your children some of the major trends in the society around you. Talk about God's leadership, presence, and power to keep.
7. Together, enjoy the adventure of new (for them) things. Make a hobby of learning about the new culture. Emphasize the beauty of cultural differences.
8. Encourage friendships.
9. Let them participate in as many decisions as possible. Encourage mature decision making with positive comments, but point out that you don't expect adult maturity from a child.
10. Encourage them to do their best, but avoid applying undue pressure.
11. Provide necessary information regarding such things as dating, sex, and different values.
12. Help the children notice styles, customs, and manners of their new homeland.
13. Make sure your family rituals don't get lost.
14. Assure them that you will always be there for them and will come to them if they need you.
15. Assure them that they can visit you back on the mission field.

Appendix D

Ways for helping MKs at *school* upon cross-cultural entry

1. Make early contact with schools the children will attend by corresponding from the field and setting up a personal interview upon arrival, in order to ensure these important things:
   a. Introduce the MK to the principal (and teacher if possible) and the school plant.
   b. Learn of school's philosophy.
   c. Explain any special needs of the MK and learn of special programs available.
   d. Volunteer your help.
   e. Demonstrate your desire for a profitable academic year for your MK.
   f. Establish rapport with individuals on the staff to ensure open and ongoing communication.
   g. Explain the school program or setting in which the child has participated.
   h. Ask for names of children in the neighborhood who could help make the transition easier.

2. Ask your pastor to introduce you to a teacher, administrator, active PTA member, or school board member who will agree to help you in knowing of school activities, political issues, availability of resources, and who would be willing to be your advocate should the need arise.

3. Ask the teacher to keep you informed about the child's progress and needs. Establish a friendly, open relationship, indicating your desire for candid discussions, since time is short.

4. Encourage your child to tell the teacher when he does not understand or is confused. Explain, however, that he should exercise good listening and work habits.

Appendix E

Ways for helping MKs at *church* upon cross-cultural entry

1. Write the pastor in advance, giving names and ages of your children, and inquiring about special programs available to them.

2. Before cross-cultural entry, help your child learn some of the frequently used hymns, choruses, Bible verses, and responses that most children will know in your home church.

3. Upon cross-cultural entry, talk with your pastor and other leaders with whom your children will be involved, explaining discretely some of the general characteristics of MKs and the special needs of your children for integration into the church family.

4. When possible, return to the same church for furloughs.

5. As much as possible, arrange for regular attendance and participation of the children in local church activities when parents are involved in deputation.

6. Have church youth groups in your home for fellowship.

7. Invite church families who have children the same ages as yours to have a meal in your home, go on a picnic together, or on an outing such as to a park or the zoo.

8. Be willing to share your mission field experiences with your child's Sunday school class or youth group.

9. Continue having family devotions in much the same way as was your family custom on the mission field. Give your children an opportunity to express their feelings about their faith, and to use part of this family time to share doubts and problems they may be having in the new environment, especially in relation to the church.

10. Be alert that your children not become overwhelmed by your too busy church life.

11. Keep joy as a major ingredient in your faith and church activities. It is sure to be contagious.

Appendix F

Ways *mission administrators* can help MKs in cross-cultural entry

1. Anticipate cross-cultural entry needs of MKs, and either provide a cross-cultural entry program or funding for such a program outside the mission.

2. Develop an on-the-field cross-cultural entry program and encourage its use before departure from the field.

3. Work with local and/or state groups in establishing a network of people, especially near college campuses with many MKs, willing to provide such things as homes for holidays.

4. Maintain contact with college administrations where there are large numbers of MKs to monitor adjustment and provide help when unusual situations arise. Avoid "big brother" network, however.

5. Have a staff person visit MKs as they reenter the home country to listen to them and help them adjust.

6. Visit or telephone the MK when possible, at least once a year—on birthdays?

7. Provide an 800 telephone number at mission headquarters to give information and assistance to the MK when needed.

8. Provide MKs with mission publications to keep them informed.

9. Issue a newsletter about and for MKs and/or a list of names and addresses of MKs in the home country.

10. During college, or after the MK's cross-cultural entry, provide at least one trip back to the mission field to visit their parents.

11. Pray regularly for them.

Appendix G

Warning signs of suicide intention

Verbal

1. Direct statements like "I want to die," or "I don't want to live anymore."
2. Indirect statements like "I want to go to sleep and never wake up," or "They'll be sorry when I'm gone," or "Soon this pain will be over."

Behavioral

1. Depression, deep sadness.
2. Lack of energy.
3. Increase or decrease in sleeping patterns.
4. Increase or decrease in appetite.
5. Impatience or impulsiveness.
6. Inability to concentrate, boredom, listlessness.
7. Anger and destructive or boisterous behavior, shifting to silent withdrawal or tearful loneliness.
8. Withdrawal from usual social activities.
9. Loss of interest in hobbies, sports, job, or school.
10. Drop in grades by a good student, or new concern about grades by a poor student.
11. Giving away possessions.
12. Making final arrangements—will, insurance, funeral.
13. Increased risk taking, e.g., driving a car recklessly.
14. Frequent accidents.
15. Previous suicide attempts.

Situational

1. Experience of a loss (through death, divorce, breakup of a relationship or loss of self-esteem).
2. Difficulty communicating with parents.
3. Problems with school or employment.
4. Drug and/or alcohol abuse.
5. Trouble with the law.

Any one of these signs by itself can be a normal part of life. To a caring observer, four or five of these signs over a two-week period should raise a red flag.

Appendix H

A true-false test about suicide

_____ 1. People who talk about killing themselves rarely commit suicide.

_____ 2. The tendency toward suicide is inherited and passes from generation to generation.

_____ 3. The suicidal person wants to die and feels that there is no turning back.

_____ 4. There is a very low correlation between alcoholism and suicide.

_____ 5. Everyone who attempts suicide, from time to time will entertain thoughts of suicide.

_____ 6. Suicidal people are mentally ill.

_____ 7. If you ask a person about his suicidal intentions, you'll encourage the person to kill himself.

_____ 8. Suicide is quite common among the lower class.

_____ 9. Suicidal people rarely seek medical attention.

_____ 10. Suicide is basically a problem that is limited to young people.

_____ 11. When a depression lifts, there is no longer any danger of suicide.

_____ 12. Suicide is a spontaneous activity that occurs without warning.

For answers turn to page 151.

Appendix J

How to tell if you are a stress-prone personality
Rate yourself as to how you typically react in each of the situations listed below. There are no right or wrong answers.

4= Always   3= Frequently   2= Sometimes   1= Never

_____ 1. Do you try to do as much as possible in the least amount of time?
_____ 2. Do you become impatient with delays or interruptions?
_____ 3. Do you have to win at games to enjoy yourself?
_____ 4. Do you find yourself speeding up the car to beat the red light?
_____ 5. Are you unlikely to ask for or indicate you need help with a problem?
_____ 6. Do you seek the admiration and respect of others?
_____ 7. Are you overly critical of the way others do their work?
_____ 8. Do you have the habit of looking at your watch or clock often?
_____ 9. Do you strive to better your position and achievements?
_____ 10. Do you spread yourself too thin in terms of your time?
_____ 11. Do you have the habit of doing more than one thing at a time?
_____ 12. Do you get irritable or angry?
_____ 13. Do you have little time for hobbies or time by yourself?
_____ 14. Do you have a tendency to talk quickly or hasten conversations?
_____ 15. Do you consider yourself hard-driving?
_____ 16. Do your friends or close relatives consider you hard-driving?
_____ 17. Do you have a tendency to get involved in multiple projects?
_____ 18. Do you have a lot of deadlines in your work?
_____ 19. Do you feel vaguely guilty and uneasy if you relax and do nothing?
_____ 20. Do you take on too many responsibilities?

_____ TOTAL

From *Life Stress* by Rosalind Forbes (1979, out of print).
Score: 20-30 Low Risk   31-55 Moderate   56-80 High Risk

This work sheet could be used as a self-help tool for both parents and MKs who will be facing the extra stress of cross-cultural entry. If scores are high, it is advisable that some changes be made in life style before changing locations.

APPENDIX H test answers: All are false.

Resources

INFORMATION ON COLLEGES AND CONTINUING EDUCATION

A's & B's of Scholarship
Octameron Press, Box 3437,
Alexandria, Va. 22302 ($4.50)

The ACT Financial Aid Services
P.O. Box 168, Iowa City, Iowa 52243
Published yearly free of cost.

The Advanced Placement Program
College Board, 45 Columbus Avenue,
New York, N.Y. 10023-6992

The Advanced Placement Offices
212-1755 Springfield Road, Kelowna,
B.C. Canada V1Y 5V5

Campus Life Magazine
Subscription Services, P.O. Box 11624,
Des Moines, Iowa 50347-1624.
Has a once-a-year listing of Christian colleges and, at times, other supplements with important college information.

The College Handbook
College Board, 45 Columbus Avenue,
New York, N.Y. 10023-6992

College Money Handbook
Peterson Guides, Princeton, N.J. 08540

Consider a Christian College
Peterson Guides, Princeton, N.J. 08540

Don't Miss Out
Octameron Press, Box 3437,
Alexandria, Va. 22302 ($4.50)

The Independent Study Catalog
Peterson's Guides, Dept. 5614,
P.O. Box 2123, Princeton, N.J. 08540

Meeting College Costs
College Bureau of Scholarship Services,
45 Columbus Ave., New York,
N.Y. 10023
Published yearly free of cost.

Moody Magazine
820 North LaSalle Drive,
Chicago, Ill. 60610-9975

Need a Lift?
American Legion Education Program,
P.O. Box 1055, Indianapolis, Ind. 46206

The Scholarship Watch
P.O. Box 7640, LaVerne, Calif. 91750

Student Guide to Financial Aid
U.S. Dept. of Education, Office of
Grants, Loans and Work Study,
Washington, D.C. 20202
Published yearly free of cost.

Writing Your College Application Essay
College Board, 45 Columbia Avenue,
New York, N.Y. 10023-6992

CORRESPONDENCE COURSES (U.S.)

A Beka Home School
Pensacola, Fla. 32523-9160
Phone: 1-800-874-BEKA
Offers three unique programs: Video
Home School, Correspondence School,
Textbooks and Material

Calvert School
Tuscany Road, Baltimore, Md. 21210
Grades K-8

International Institute, Inc.
N6128 Sawyer Lake Road, White Lake,
Wis. 54491
Grades K-8

Missionary Accelerated Christian Education (MACE)
P.O. Box 1438, 2600 ACE Lane,
Lewisville, Texas 75067-1438
Phone (214) 462-1776
Grades K-12

Pensacola Christian Correspondence School
125 S. John St., Pensacola, Fla. 32503
Grades Nursery-9

Science Research Associates, Inc.
259 E. Erie St., Chicago, Ill. 60611
Grades 9-12

University of California
Extension Education Department, Dept. of Correspondence Instruction,
Berkeley, Calif. 94720
Grades 9-12

University of Maryland
University Extension Division,
College Park, Md. 20742
Grades 9-12

University of Nebraska
Lincoln High School Independent University Extension Division,
Lincoln, Neb. 68508
Grades 9-12

University of North Dakota
Division of Independent Study, State University Station, Fargo, N.D. 58102
Grades 9-12

CORRESPONDENCE COURSES
(Canada)
Alberta Dept. of Education
Correspondence Courses Division,
Executive Bldg., Jasper Ave. & 109 St.,
Edmonton, Alberta T5N 3M8

British Columbia Dept. of Education
Correspondence Course Division,
Parliament Bldgs., Victoria, B.C.
V8V 1X4

Manitoba Dept. of Education
Correspondence Course Division,
1181 Portage Ave., Winnipeg, Manitoba
R3G 0T3

New Brunswick Dept. of Education
Correspondence Course Division,
Box 6000, Fredericton, N.B. E3B 5H1

Newfoundland Dept. of Education
Correspondence Course Division,
Box 578, Halifax, N.S. B3J 2S9

Ontario Dept. of Education
Correspondence Course Division,
Ministry of Education, Mowat Block,
Queen's Park, Toronto, Ontario
M7A 1L2

Prince Edward Island Dept. of Education
Correspondence Course Division,
Box 2000, Charlottetown, Prince Edward Island C1A 7N8

Quebec Dept. of Education
Correspondence Course Division,
Bldg. G, Cite Parlementaire,
Quebec City, P.Q. G1R 5A5

Saskatchewan Dept. of Education
Correspondence Course Division,
2220 College Ave, Parkview Place,
Regina, Saskatchewan S4P 2Y8

LEARNING DISABILITIES
Texas Scottish Rites Hospital for Crippled Children
2222 Welborn St., Dallas, Texas 75219
Offers set of 355 instructional videos for learning-disabled children.

Jemicy School
11 Celadon Rd., Owings Mills,
Md. 21117
(301) 653-2700

National Institute for Learning Disabilities (NILD)
107 Seekel St., Norfolk, Va 23505
(804) 423-8646 Testing and diagnosis are often available at international schools abroad.

EDUCATIONAL EVALUATION
Interfaces (International Family and Children's Educational Services)
Mrs. Kathryn Burnes, P.O. Box 11233,
Richmond, Va. 23230-1233
(804) 794-4064

153

CROSS-CULTURAL ENTRY PROGRAMS

Interaction, Inc., RD 1, Box 199A, Vorheesville, N.Y. 12186
(518) 872-1936   Fax: (518) 872-1812

Interfaces (International Family and Children's Educational Services)
Mrs. Kathryn Burnes, P.O. Box 11233, Richmond, Va. 23230-1233
(804) 794-4064

Narramore Christian Foundation
P.O. Box 5000, Rosemead, Calif. 91770
(818) 288-7000

Quest (A Wycliffe program for North Americans who are interested in overseas mission work.) 19891 Beach Blvd., Huntington Beach, Calif. 92647
(714) 536-9346 or (800) 388-1928

COUNSELORS

Barnabas International
Jim and Ruth Lauer, P.O. Box 1388, DeSoto, Texas 75115   (214) 230-1710

Fairhaven Ministries
Route 2, Box 1022, Roan Mountain, Tenn. 37687   (615) 542-5332

Interaction, Inc.
RD 1, Box 199A, Vorheesville, N.Y. 12186
(518) 872-1936   Fax: (518) 872-1812
The Christian Medical Society and the Christian Legal Society may be contacted through Interaction, Inc. for medical and lawyer services.

Interfaces (International Family and Children's Educational Services)
Mrs. Kathryn Burnes, P.O. Box 11233, Richmond, Va. 23230-1233
(804) 794-4064

Link Care Center
1734 West Shaw Ave., Fresno, Calif. 93711   (209) 439-5920

Missionary Family Counseling Services
Doris Walters, Pastoral Counselor, 208 Oakwood Square, Winston-Salem, N.C. 27103
(919) 724-0964

Missionary Internship
P.O. Box 50110, Colorado Springs, Colo. 80949
(719) 594-0687   Fax: (719) 594-4682

Narramore Christian Foundation
P.O. Box 5000, Rosemead, Calif. 91770
(818) 288-7000

READING AND VIDEO RESOURCES

Austin, Clyde N. *Cross-Cultural Reentry: An Annotated Bibliography.* (Abilene, Texas: Abilene Christian University Press, 1983).

Austin, Clyde N. *Cross-Cultural Reentry: A Book of Readings.* (Abilene, Texas: Abilene Christian University Press, 1986).

Burkett, Larry. *Get A Grip On Your Money.* Student Text and Teacher's Guide. (Colorado Springs, Colo.: Focus on the Family Publishing, 1990).

College Planning. *College Planning/ Search Book.* ACT Publications, P.O. Box 168, Iowa City, Iowa 52243. Yearly editions.

Compendium of the International Conference on Missionary Kids (Manila 1984): New Directions in Missions: Implications for MKs. 1984. Distributed by: Missionary Internship, Box 50110, Colorado Springs, Colo. 80949-0110, and by ICMK Office, P.O. Box 960, Northport, Ala. 35476.

Echerd, Pam and Arathoon, Alice, editors. *Compendium of the International Conference on Missionary Kids* (Quito, Ecuador, January 4-8, 1987). Volume I: *Understanding and Nurturing the Missionary Family.* Volume II: *Planning for MK Nurture.* William Carey Library, Pasadena, Calif. 1989. Distributed by: Missionary Internship, P.O. Box 50110, Colorado Springs, Colo. 80949-0110, and by ICMK Office, P.O.Box 960, North-port, Ala. 35476.

Elkind, David. *All Grown Up and No Place to Go (Teenagers in Crisis).* (Reading, Mass.: Addison Wesley Publishing Company, 1984).

Ervin, Nancy. *Kids on the Move.* (Birmingham, Mich.: Conquest Corporation, 1988). P.O. Box 1090, Birmingham, Mich. 48012. The book is accompanied by the pamphlet "Straight Talk About Moving... One Teen to Another.")

Foyle, Marjory F. *Overcoming Missionary Stress.* (Wheaton, Ill.: Evangelical Missions Information Service, 1989).

Grimbol, William R. *Why Should I Care?* (Minneapolis, Minn.: Augsburg Publishing House, 1988).

Herbert, Martin. *Living with Teenagers.* (New York: Basil Blackwell Inc., 1987). 432 Park Ave. South, Suite 1503, New York, N.Y. 10016.

Kachur, Robert M., editor. *The Complete Campus Companion* (Downers Grove, Ill.: InterVarsity Press, 1988).

Krefetz, Gerald. *How to Pay for Your Children's College Education.* College Board, 45 Columbus Avenue, New York, N.Y. 10023-6992.

Lawhead, Alice and Steve. *The Ultimate Student Handbook.* (Wheaton, Ill.: Crossway Books, 1983).

Lerner, Richard M. and Galambos, Nancy L. *Experiencing Adolescence: A Sourcebook for Parents, Teachers, and Teens.* (New York, N.Y.: Garland Publishing, Inc., 1984). 36 Madison Ave., New York, N.Y. 10016.

Lockerbie, D. Bruce. *Education of Missionaries' Children: The Neglected Dimension of World Mission.* (Pasadena, Calif.: William Carey Library, 1975).

Loss, Myron. *Culture Shock.* (Winona Lake, Ind.: Light and Life Press, 1983).

McDowell, Josh and Day, Dick. *Why Wait?* (San Bernardino, Calif.: Here's Life Publisher, Inc., 1987). P.O. Box 1576, San Bernadino, Calif. 92402.

Miller, Gordon Porter. *Choosing a College.* (The Student's Step-by-Step Decision-Making Workbook). (New York, N.Y.: The College Board, 1990). 45 Columbus Ave., New York, N.Y. 10023-6992.

Moody Video. *It's Worth Waiting For.* With Greg Spek. Set of two videos: 1. *Some Straight Talk About Sex* and *Petting, Pinching* and *Peer Pressure.* 2. *Why Not* and *Perversions and Preventions.* (Companion book by Moody Press). 1988.

O'Donnell, Kelly and Michele. *Helping Missionaries Grow.* (Pasadena, Calif.: William Carey Library, 1988).

Osman, Betty, *Learning Disabilities: A Family Affair.* (New York: Random House, 1979).

Peters, Daniel Barth. *Rookies: An Activity Book for Families Going to the Mission Field*. (Fresno, Calif.: Link Care Center, 1985) 1734 West Shaw Ave., Fresno, Calif. 93711.

Rowen, Ruth and Samuel. *Sojourners. The Family on the Move*. (Farmington, Mich.: Associates of Urbanus, 1990).

Schimmels, Cliff. *When Junior High Invades Your Home*. (Old Tappan, N.J.: Flemming H. Revell Company, 1984).

Schimmels, Mary P. *Kids of the Kingdom. A Working Bibliography on Missionary Kids*. (Wheaton, Ill.: Evangelical Missions Information Service, 1991). Box 794, Wheaton, Ill. 60189.

Sharmat, Marjorie W. *Gile Monsters Meet You at the Airport*. (New York, N.Y.: Macmillan Publishing Company, 1980).

Sherman, Dean. *Relationships*. A series of six videos. 1. *God Created Two Sexes;* 2. *God's Gift of Attraction;* 3. *God's Logical Loving Limits;* 4. *Reasons For Wrong Relations;* 5. *Morals: God's Point of View;* 6. *Philosophies For Dating*. (U. N. Video, 75-5851, Kuakini Hwy., Kailua-Kona, Hawaii 96740.) 1989.

Stevens, Suzanne. *Classroom Success for the Learning Disabled*. (Winston-Salem, N.C.: John F. Blair Publisher, 1984). 1406 Plaza Drive, Winston-Salem, N.C. (800) 222-9796.

Stevens, Suzanne. *The Learning Disabled Child: Ways that Parents Can Help*. (Winston-Salem, N.C.: John F. Blair Publisher, 1984).

Troutman, Charles. *Everything You Want to Know About the Mission Field, But Are Afraid You Won't Learn Until You Get There*. (Downers Grove, Ill.: InterVarsity Press, 1976).

U.S. Department of Education. *Growing Up Drug Free: A Parent's Guide to Prevention*. Washington, D.C., 1989. Distributed by National Clearinghouse for Alcohol and Drug Information, P.O.Box 2345, Rockville, Md. 20852. Free.

Van Reken, Ruth E. *Letters I Never Sent*. (Published by "Letters," P.O. Box 90084, Indianapolis, Ind. 46290-0084. (317) 251-4933) 1986.

Viser, William C. *It's OK to Be an MK*. (Nashville, Tenn.: Broadman Press, 1986).

Walters, Doris. *An Assessment of Reentry Issues of the Children of Missionaries*. (208 Oakwood Sq., Winston-Salem, N.C. 27103) 1991.

Ward, Ted. *Living Overseas*. A Book of Preparations. (New York, N.Y.: The Free Press, 1984).

MISCELLANEOUS

Interact
Occasional articles about MKs.
P.O. Box 863, Wheaton, Ill. 60189

Mu Kappa International
P.O.Box 1388, DeSoto, Texas 75115
(See Appendix A.)

Overseas Ministries Study Center (OMSC)
490 Prospect Street, New Haven, Conn. 06511-2196
(203) 624-6672
Hosts a yearly seminar on meeting the special needs of MKs.

Index

266.0083
G6622

96593

3 4711 00087 2822